Public School Finance Decoded

Public School Finance Decoded

A Straightforward Approach to Linking the Budget to Student Achievement

Jay C. Toland

PUBLISHED IN PARTNERSHIP WITH THE
ASSOCIATION OF SCHOOL BUSINESS OFFICIALS

ROWMAN & LITTLEFIELD
Lanham • Boulder • New York • London

Published in partnership with the Association of School Business Officials

Published by Rowman & Littlefield
A wholly owned subsidiary of The Rowman & Littlefield Publishing Group, Inc.
4501 Forbes Boulevard, Suite 200, Lanham, Maryland 20706
www.rowman.com

Unit A, Whitacre Mews, 26-34 Stannary Street, London SE11 4AB

Copyright © 2017 by Jay C. Toland

All rights reserved. No part of this book may be reproduced in any form or by any electronic or mechanical means, including information storage and retrieval systems, without written permission from the publisher, except by a reviewer who may quote passages in a review.

British Library Cataloguing in Publication Information Available

Library of Congress Cataloging-in-Publication Data

Names: Toland, Jay C., 1975– author.
Title: Public school finance decoded : a straightforward approach to linking the budget to student achievement / Jay C. Toland.
Description: Lanham : Rowman & Littlefield, [2017]
Identifiers: LCCN 2016027765 (print) | LCCN 2016030950 (ebook) |
  ISBN 9781475827675 (cloth : alk. paper) | ISBN 9781475827682 (pbk. : alk. paper) |
  ISBN 9781475827699 (electronic)
Subjects: LCSH: Public schools—United States—Finance. |
  Academic achievement—United States.
Classification: LCC LB2825 .T62 2016 (print) | LCC LB2825 (ebook) |
  DDC 379.1220973—dc23
LC record available at https://lccn.loc.gov/2016027765

∞™ The paper used in this publication meets the minimum requirements of American National Standard for Information Sciences—Permanence of Paper for Printed Library Materials, ANSI/NISO Z39.48-1992.

Printed in the United States of America

I would like to thank God for all the wonderful things he has blessed my family with.

I would also like to thank my brilliant and wildly successful wife Mackenzie for her support, as well as all of those that have helped me through years.

I would also like to thank the people that helped me professionally:

Dr. Freddie Williamson
Dr. Randy Bridges
Dr. Ron Hargrave
Cory Satterfield
Larry Johnson
Dr. Valerie Williams
Wannaa Chavis
Rick Stout
Tony Messer
Pam Satterfield

The Finance Department at Scotland County Schools—Debbie Lawrence, Tennillia Oxendine, Larissa York, Donna McQueen, Victoria Blue, and Linda Smith

Finally, everyone associated with Rowman & Littlefield Publishing Group, especially Tom Koerner, Bethany Janka, and Anita Singh.

Contents

Preface	ix
Introduction	1
1 How Finance and Student Achievement Go Hand in Hand	3
2 Looking at the Past to Predict the Future	15
3 How to Use District Efficiency Indicators	23
4 What Expenses to Include in the Indicators	31
5 Child Nutrition Ratios	39
6 Maintenance and Operation of Plant Ratios	49
7 Transportation Ratios	57
8 Technology Ratios	65
9 Other Ratios to Consider	75
10 What Expenditures Directly Correlate with Student Achievement	83
11 Linking the Strategic Plan to Budget	91
12 How It All Fits Together	97
About the Author	105

Preface

It had been bothering me for months. How can CFOs from big companies have such a huge say in their company's performance, whereas a CFO from a school district is sometimes viewed as a "head bookkeeper"?

I needed to figure out what a school district's CFO could contribute to the conversation about student achievement that was not being contributed currently. How could the CFOs get a seat at the table?

I knew there had to be a way to predict student achievement by using financial information. I would sit in all those meetings where different stakeholders would talk about different data points, and what they thought they meant. I knew the key was being *proactive* instead of being *reactive*: How could I help the superintendent understand which schools were not going to perform well before the results actually happened?

I started to brainstorm about what actually contributes to student achievement. Once I had these attributes laid out, I dissected each one of them to see how money contributed to them. I then started to measure and present on them.

The feedback I received was good. It was a way for educators who really had no financial background to understand how finance works and contributes to student achievement. Everyone realized that finance processes payroll and pays vendors and that finance is audited, but they did not realize how finance had a wealth of valuable information. Even the data available at the school level can be used to start a conversation about what the school purchases and uses, and how that contributes to the district's mission of educating children.

Those items, whether related to payroll or for goods and services, are where the data for student achievement lie. It is an ability to be able to look at expenditure and see what was actually purchased, and how these purchases contribute to student achievement. In for-profit businesses, every purchase is rated on what it adds to the bottom line. In school districts, the bottom line is the level of student achievement.

This book shows you how to measure the things that relate to student achievement directly. It also looks at departments that could be adjusted to save money, which can be funneled into curriculum and instruction to directly benefit the students.

In some states there is an all-out war against public schools. We need to show our constituents and stakeholders that we can use the resources for good and how a good investment in public education is an economic stimulator.

I hope this book helps you understand how important public school finance is and how, by understanding public school finance, a school district can gain a competitive advantage. I appreciate you taking the time to read this book. The fact that you are reading this book shows your dedication to the students you serve, and I hope and pray that this book serves you to help these children.

Introduction

This book is organized to naturally flow to complete one's understanding of the relationship between student achievement and finance. In the beginning, the book presents the foundation to a greater understanding of how significant the data from finance can be.

There is always a need for more money. Many times in school districts the ability to generate new revenue or new money is next to impossible and focusing on that takes away from the vision and mission of the district itself. Therefore, it is prudent to look at existing programs and how money can be saved to create new money.

One of the underlying concepts is that the past can be used to predict the future. Therefore, in chapter 2, the concept of using the past to predict the future is laid out in detail.

The expenditures should be universal between most school districts, and a keen recognition of the audited financial statements has been given. As the reader goes through this book, they should use their own district's data to follow along. The numbers that are required are inherently simple.

Having an overall progress report for the district is important for the high-level decision makers, and this topic is introduced next, with a continued emphasis on simplicity. It is important to make sure the financial health of the district is stable before moving forward with any analysis.

Painting the picture for the large programs, where there is a lot of opportunity to create savings, is next. There are certain items that hold the key to predicting student achievement, and there are other expenditures that lead to higher efficiency.

The large programs are explored next; these programs usually fall under the umbrella of auxiliary services. These programs, which are typically required by the district but are not directly related to the core value of student enrichment, provide indirect support and tend to cost a lot of money.

Expanding the tool kit to look at other programs is an exciting step. These other programs can be controlled by adding money or taking money away, and it is important to understand what this does to the significance of the program.

Finally, this book presents a detailed look at the road map of the district and outlines how the budget and agendas should match the road map or strategic plan. It is vitally important to look at the strategic plan and put the planned expenditures next to each goal. Creating and publishing the budget and putting next to each line item what goal that particular line item contributes provides stakeholders an understanding of the financial expenditures from the strategic plan document and the budget document.

The book closes with a summary that brings everything together. This summary helps the reader understand how to use the information presented to ultimately increase student achievement.

Chapter 1

How Finance and Student Achievement Go Hand in Hand

OVERVIEW

This chapter presents a brief introduction to this book. Descriptions on how to use past performance data, create parameters for success, find the data needed, and differentiate between monitoring and predictive ratios to help convert financial data to predict student performance have also been discussed.

INTRODUCTION

It is prudent that the finance department takes part in the conversation about educating a child. The finance department is home to all the expenditure data for the district. Within that expenditure data lies the path to the future.

A school system can communicate its academic performance through its expenditure, not only by its current but also by its past transactions. The finance department can at the minimum provide the information to connect the dots between money and student achievement.

The best-case scenario is where the finance department can lead the way to showcasing the district's expenditures and advise district leaders what they can expect through the analysis of the expenditures. Furthermore, the finance department should be housing the data accurately (tested through an annual audit) so that the predictions are accurate.

The process of reviewing financial data to predict student achievement should follow the process of planning, spending, collecting, separating, analyzing, and communicating the expenditure data.

Planning involves the preparation of the strategic plan and the budget. These two documents need to be prepared hand in hand, so that they can stand on their own as a complete document and tell the story of the other document at the same time. In other words, the strategic plan should reference the budget and vice versa.

Spending is the fun part; there are two keys to spending: doing it correctly, of course, and doing it in a transparent manner. Transparency is necessary because it is important, as stewards of tax payers' money, to be clear about what the actual purchases are, who they were made from, and how much they cost.

A school district is always in the need of additional funds. The key to getting more money is being able to provide an accurate account of how existing funds were spent.

Collecting is the process of archiving the expenditure data and providing access to all who need the data. It may be in the form of online reporting or an easy system to request documentation. Regardless of the system employed, there needs to be a clear process on how the expenditure data are accessed.

Separating is the process of gathering the expense data that predicts student achievement from the expenditure data; the expense data is used to ensure whether the district is running efficiently.

The non-predictive expenditures can interfere with the necessary expenditures (those that deal with specific teaching and learning) due to a finite amount of resources.

Analyzing is all about crunching the numbers to see the story they tell. A district can use its expenditure data to either benchmark against itself or against another district of similar demographics. That process of comparing is to decipher if there are any variances or differences which need to be addressed.

Analyzing also entails figuring out what the expenditure data is predicting. When analyzing the data, it is critical to look at the actual objective or purpose of the expenditure and to measure if that objective or purpose is aligned with that particular expenditure. It is also a process of compiling the district's efficiency indicators which tells a story about the efficiency of services that the district has to participate in and if any savings can be realized throughout the operations of these necessary services.

Communicating is the process of providing the final product to the necessary stakeholders through any medium available. The process also takes into consideration the necessity of simplicity and the end user of the data.

Empathy is important because it enables the person compiling the information to forecast any questions the end user may ask. With that forecasting ability, a more complete service will be provided.

It is very interesting to see how difficult computation of public school finance can be, and how problematic it can be to get any relevant data that is not related to an audit. Performing exceptionally on an audit is imperative because that opens up grant opportunities for the district, and districts with mediocre audits may not be eligible for grants.

It is also critical to be able to show the public that the school district can properly spend the funds it receives, achieve a satisfactory bond rating, and build relationships with stakeholders. However, there is more to public school finance than just the audit.

Let's look at corporate finance: many of those who have ever dabbled with investing know what a price-to-earnings ratio is. However, for others who may not know what it means, for simplicity's sake, the definition is as follows: it is the rate at which the market (buyers and sellers of stocks) is willing to pay for future growth.

The higher the ratio, the more the market is willing to pay for the growth of the company. The actual calculation is the price of the stock divided by the earnings per share of the stock; once that division is done, boom, there is the ratio. This ratio can lead to a host of other questions: Why is it low? Why is it high? What are the price-to-earnings ratios of companies in the same space? The important point here is to see how relatively simple the calculation is and how it opens the door to a host of questions and opportunities.

Furthermore, this ratio offers a great deal of insight on how the market perceives the stock. This ratio helps many investors when making sound investment decisions. It is important that when dealing with complex tasks, simple arithmetic can provide a relatively effective metric that is easy to understand.

This example illustrates the necessity of simplicity in a complex environment. Many educators have no idea where the money goes in running a school district or, for that matter, where the money came from. Their number one goal is to educate children.

There is a simple way to look at how funds are spent and if those expenditures not only align with the vision and mission of the district but also are being focused on student achievement.

This book will achieve that simplicity by not only providing simple, straightforward calculations and ratios on how to monitor a school district's performance but also helping predict student achievement, much like how a benchmark test can help predict a student's performance on an end of grade assessment.

To further illustrate the need for simplicity in public school finance, that education touches almost everyone and not just in the sense that almost everyone has gone to school, but, on the same note, almost everyone helps pay for it with their share of taxes. Furthermore, some school districts are the largest employers in their respective communities.

It is necessary to defend school districts and the complex world they operate in because they are like conglomerate organizations, where they are a fleet of buses, cafeterias, buildings, classrooms, and expected to be on the cutting edge of technology. Some parts of the school district are set up to be run like a for-profit business, whereas other parts are required to spend the fund allotted to them and if they need more money, they are instructed to request for it.

Usually a school district needs to transport and feed its customers (students) before it even begins its core business: teaching and learning. However, within those programs lie integral details and facets that can help lead to increased student achievement by monitoring its respective financial performance.

The information center for the financial data of the district is the finance department.

Common practices for a CFO and the finance office of a school district usually are as follows:

- Time and attendance—The recording and processing of the absences, clocking in and out, and federal labor standards act data for the district (can be thousands of employees).
- Process—Payroll (paying staff) and accounts payable (paying the vendors for the supplies and materials that the district needs to run day to day and carry out its strategic plan).
- Record holder—The finance office usually holds deeds, contracts, and records. Some programs require the storage of data up to seven years.
- Audit—The finance department is the facilitator of the audit and the audit has several nonfinancial parts; in North Carolina it is concussion data for sports teams and Pre-K physical data, to just name a few.
- Catch all—When a superintendent requires specific data or needs a high level of precision in a project, he or she usually turns to the finance department, opening the department up to many time-consuming and unplanned events. However, these needs ensure job security.
- Allocation of staff—The majority of expenditures for a school district comes from personnel. The finance department, along with the human resources department, calculates and allocates the staff to the different schools and departments within a school district.

PAST PERFORMANCE

The finance department has a wealth of past performance data. The validity of this data is tested from a compliance point of view by an audit firm. The audit firm especially hones in with local, state, and/or federal laws.

The financial data is also used as a reporting mechanism: how much money does the district have, where does the district spend the money, when did the district receive its money, and a snapshot of where it may spend its money in the future.

We can use this past performance to contribute to a baseline on how student performance is related to financial performance. For example, if a school spent $3,200 in one fiscal year in substitute funds and the school performed well, then $3,200 may be a good baseline for next year. However, a flag should arise if halfway through the year they spend $3,600. This flag should lead to an investigation of the specific absence of data (as in the case of Main St. Elementary in table 1.1), looking at specific teachers and the quality of the substitute teacher that is in the particular classroom.

The increase in absences could be for a variety of reasons: maternity leave, short-term disability, or illness. The source for such an increase could be from only two or three teachers. However, if there are long-term absences, it is important to investigate the quality of the substitute teacher to make sure the rigor is still being delivered in the classroom.

The trick here is that a district may track absence data, but a vacancy may not trigger a change in the attendance percentage. Therefore, if a superintendent or a high-ranking official just scans the absence data, he or she may not see a flag, but if he or she looks at the substitute teacher cost data, it would raise a flag, and special attention could be given to the particular classrooms that are incurring the additional costs (as in the case of Pine St. Elementary in table 1.2).

In table 1.3, there is a variance in the difference between the number of days missed and the substitute expenditure data (Lake St. Elementary). This variance could be from vacancies and needs to be investigated. The purpose of the investigation should be to make sure the vacancies are posted if there are good hiring practices at the school level.

Table 1.1   Certified—Require a Substitute Teacher—12.31.2017

	Elm St. Elem.		Main St. Elem.		North Elem.	
School	FY 2016	12.31.2017	FY 2016	12.31.2017	FY 2016	12.31.2017
Sub expense YTD ($)	10,200.00	3,500.00	3,200.00	3,600.00	6,600.00	6,500.00

*Substitute teacher costs $100 per day.

Table 1.2   Absence % and Substitute Teacher Expense

School	Pine St. Elem.		South St. Elem.		West St. Elem.	
Year	2016	2017	2016	2017	2016	2017
Absence (%)	96	96	98	98	95	97
Sub expense YTD ($)	7,100.00	10,200.00	3,200.00	3,600.00	6,600.00	6,500.00
Number of certified staff members	20	20	18	20	15	17
Total days missed	67	65	30	34	63	43

Table 1.3   Certified—Require a Substitute Teacher—12.31.2016

School	Lake St. Elem..	Oak St. Elem.	North Elem.	South Middle School	North Middle School	Central High School
Absence (%)	96	98	95	99	97	96
Sub Exp. YTD* ($)	10,200	3,200	6,600	1,900	7,100	18,100
Number of certified staff members	20	18	15	24	26	45
Total days missed	67	30	63	20	66	151

*YTD, as of 12.31.2016

Table 1.4   Comparing School Grades to Staff Development Expenses

School	Elm St. Elem.	Main St. Elem.	North Elem.
School Grade	A	C	D
Staff Dev. Exp. ($)	15,423.00	345.00	415.00

Existing data can be used to try and pinpoint strategic maximization of expenditure data. If a district or a specific school experiences success and there is a similar district or school, then one could compare financial data. For example, if the successful school spent more on a staff development program than a school that was not as successful (table 1.4) with the same demographics, that would open the door to investigating what staff development program the successful school participated in.

Furthermore, one must investigate what model was used to deliver the staff development program. For example, train the trainer, where the successful school may have sent a handful of high fliers and then asked those high fliers to go to a number of staff development programs and then bring back and deliver the information at the appropriate staff meeting.

Without analyzing the expenditure data, it would not be inherent to look at the specific elements that contributed to the school's success because there is no specific matrix that will look at how many staff development programs a school had participated in.

If a district can establish trust between itself and its stakeholders by using a method to report past financial data in a clearly understandable manner, it would be a huge step forward. It is important to realize that individuals may not agree with a certain decision, but if they are given all the elements that contributed to the decision, they may develop empathy, and that empathy can contribute to understanding, and finally trust will happen.

Once that trust is created, a relationship will be formed which will lead to collaboration, which in turn leads to cooperation and growth.

Innovation can truly happen with past performance data through simply building baselines, investigating variances, and converting that data into an understandable format which will lead to future relationships and achieve the end goal of student achievement through cooperation and collaboration.

PARAMETERS FOR SUCCESS

To use financial data to monitor and predict student achievement, it is critical to have certain parameters in place. This can be compared to having the correct address keyed into a GPS or smartphone for directions. If the initial data or directions are not accurate, then the destination will also not be accurate, and at the end of the analysis or trip, it may be even more confusing than the beginning because the correct destination was not reached.

There are three parameters for success to use financial data for student achievement. The first parameter is having expenditures coded or labeled to the correct physical location.

Table 1.5 provides an example of a budget code. Each piece of equipment or service provided is linked to a specific sequence of number in a predetermined format, that is, a budget code assigned to it. The correct physical location is the "Location" section or 343 (this represents a specific school number).

The second parameter is having the expenditures labeled to the proper purpose: Were the supplies purchased for instructional or noninstructional use? The number in the "Purpose" column designates whether the expenditure is instructional or noninstructional, even though the majority of expenditures can be traced directly to the students. The expenses that coded directly to instructional are without a doubt traceable directly to the student.

The third parameter is simplicity. The process of communicating financial data across wide areas or groups of people is difficult; it can be compared to going to the doctor's office, and when a doctor is describing something, he or she obviously uses words from the English language; the patient may understand what words the doctor is literally using, but they may not actually comprehend what the doctor is saying.

Perhaps if a doctor were to incorporate common and simple language, everyone would be better off. To be able to communicate the message with simplicity is the key to comprehension.

To achieve the first two parameters, it is imperative to use the audit report and financial statements. These reports are prepared every year by an independent audit firm. Think of the audit report and financial statements as an invitation or itinerary for traveling.

Those documents have key information to make sure the parameters for success are in place or that the destination is accurate. When observing the audit report, look for any audit findings that may have arisen from misappropriation

Table 1.5 Sample Budget Code

2	5110	001	121	343	000	00
Fund source	Purpose	Report code	Object	Location	Optional	Optional

of funds, question costs, and/or inaccurate coding. These findings are usually listed toward the back of the audit report and are separated by fund.

The reason this is important is because accurate data is needed to translate the numbers into simplistic ratios and percentages. For example, for every transaction there should be some sort of designation to the location of the expenditure, whether it is a maintenance garage or a high school. These location designations are very important.

Ordinarily the financial statements do not drill down to the specific location; however, if the audit reports have a clean bill of health for the district, then it is highly likely that the location data is accurately embedded into the transactions.

Furthermore, accuracy is very important, and much like the location data, the audit report will speak of the accuracy of the data and expenditures. The necessity of the accuracy is imperative because it is easy to label or code something incorrectly. For example, is a staff development program expenditure for guidance counselors or school nurses?

The person at the site level who is responsible to submit the documentation for payment may not be sure and he or she may label it incorrectly. Once it reaches the finance department for payment, the department may process it and not follow through to make sure the expenditure is labeled correctly.

Therefore, if a comparison is made year after year on the expenditure data and the baseline year was coded correctly and the second year incorrectly, there probably would be a variance, and it may be an unnecessary variance because, in actuality, the spending, if it was coded correctly, may be the same year after year.

Finally simplicity is the key to effective comprehension and implementation. Like any major shift or change, there needs to be collaboration at the school level. For example, when a school is creating their strategic plan, they should include all of the stakeholders. In the same fashion when describing the process of converting financial data into data used to predict student achievement, it is important to be fed back on what should be monitored. Within that process simplicity is key.

When reporting the financial data, simplicity is the catalyst to help the end user to be able to easily process the information and focus on improving or sustaining success. For example, looking at two numbers and determining which one is higher and knowing that the higher the better is simple.

Presentation of data can add to simplicity, whether in a chart or using red for negative numbers (because it is universal that red is bad) to clearly illustrate the trend of the data. The key to actually coming full circle is simplicity and being able to make quick decisions from simple and accurate data.

DATA GALORE

Data-driven decisions are more than educational buzzwords; it can be a way of life for some school districts. This concept makes perfect sense; there are several clichés that talk about telling the future with the past and that is the core idea behind making data-driven decisions. The finance office has a plethora of data. The best part of the equation is that the data should be accurate and easily sortable.

The next step is to relate the financial data into something useful for all stakeholders to analyze and understand. This concept will be covered in greater detail in chapter 10, but it is important to start with the conclusion in mind.

A detailed example would be to look at a school with a high at-risk population. In order to look to improve student achievement, the conversation would begin with how to improve student achievement at an at-risk school. One answer could be consistency; research talks about how at-risk children need consistency to be successful. What does consistency look like to a student? The walk around answer is, *the same teacher every day*. How can financial data be used to see if a teacher is present every day?

Even though it is not always useful to answer a question with a question, this time it works. What is needed if a teacher is not present? A substitute teacher. What does a substitute teacher need? He or she needs to be paid; therefore, there is a tangible cost associated with the teacher not being present: the actual cost of the substitute teacher.

Therefore, by creating a baseline for the substitute teacher cost and then comparing that baseline to the current year, an explanation can be created.

If the cost gets higher year after year, then more attention should be given to teacher attendance; on the other hand, attention could be given to vacancies as well. (If vacancies are the case, attention needs to be given to recruitment not absenteeism.)

This process can be viewed through the eyes of a family that wants to strengthen its bond together. A bond can be strengthened by spending quality time together. A way to measure is to look at the amount of hours the parents' work and/or the amount of time the family spends apart from each other.

One way a family can measure the amount of time available by reconciling the amounts of days the parents have taken off of work compared to the same time a year ago. The number of days gone up or down tells the story of the availability of opportunity to spend quality time together.

Another example would be ensuring the performance of a high-performing school. The conclusion would be how to sustain or build on the high performance. It would be useful to look at the previous expenditures from the years where the high performance has been happening. The simplest way to look at this data and eliminate things that will make this data confusing would be to look at the expenditures on a per-pupil basis or as a percentage of total expenditures.

Once computed, the per-pupil amount can simply be set in a graph or analyzed to see if there are any changes. If there are changes, then investigate those further on a case-by-case basis. The key is to realize the simplicity and the innovation by adding this method, of analyzing expenditure data on a per-pupil basis, to a tool box of other elements such as benchmark tests and student attendance data to predict student achievement.

MONITORING OR PREDICTIVE

Expenditures can be grouped into two when looking at student performance: a monitoring group and a predictive group. The monitoring groups look mainly at the different services performed outside of teaching and learning but are critical to the day-to-day operations of a school district, whereas the predictive group looks at the expenditures related to teaching and learning.

The importance of the monitoring group is flexibility. To make sure there is flexibility and, more importantly, liquidity (having access to cash or a cash substitute), it is important to observe the monitoring group.

This is because this group of expenditures, if not monitored, can balloon and take up more funds than allotted. The kicker is these expenditures must be carried out; therefore, the expenditures will need to happen on continuous basis. These expenditures can include, but are not limited to, child nutrition, transportation, and maintenance.

It is important to establish the connection between flexibility and, for example, an abrupt increase in transportation costs. If there is a rise in transportation costs, then those expenditures will pull funds from other sources and possibly take way from other goals that may have been identified as strategic ones and critical for the district's success.

However, if there is monitoring, then this should not happen, especially if this analysis happens early in the fiscal year, when almost anything can be managed, as opposed to being in the second semester and needing to freeze spending to transfer funds from other budgets to cover overages in the problem/unexpected areas.

For example, if there is a leaky pipe under a place of residence, and the owner is unaware of the leak, the owner will receive a higher than expected water bill and will need to come up with the funds from other places, savings, or less critical places in the household budget, to cover the expense of the lost water.

An even worse scenario happens if the bill is on some sort of auto payment where the amount is automatically deducted from a bank account. If no attention is given to the water bill over time, it will take a check to bounce to bring attention to this matter of the leaky pipe. How often are budgets at the school level ignored for months at a time by non-finance administrators?

The predicative indicators are calculations that, by their nature, can help predict future outcomes. This happens because the expenditures have been identified as ones that are associated with certain things that can predict and/or are important to student achievement.

For example, a well-known factor that leads to student achievement is parent engagement. How can parent engagement be measured? One way of measurement is through expenses incurred to host parents at a school. At times parents need to be motivated to visit a school and with that motivation comes an expenditure.

The word "engagement" might mislead because true engagement might not exist if the parent is just present for free food; however, it is a step in the right direction if the parent had not been present before.

Within federal funding, there is specific funding embedded for parent engagement. With that said, if the year-to-date expenditures are looked up, and there have been zero or very little spent on parent engagement, then it can be deduced that student performance may suffer at that particular school for which the expenditure data was pulled because there is no expenditure data for parent engagement.

SUMMARY

This chapter introduced the concepts that will be covered in this book. It is important to realize the need for simplicity of data when it is being communicated. Furthermore, along with processing payroll and paying vendors, simplicity should be a major function of the finance department.

The finance department is the keeper of the financial data and that data is audited once a year from an outside source to ensure accuracy.

When predicting student achievement, the path can begin by using data that has already happened; that data can be used to paint the picture of what can happen.

Transparency is a critical step to predict student achievement because all known expenditures need to be identified when calculating ratios or analyzing financial data.

The three parameters for success for predicting student achievement are (1) having the expenditures coded to the proper location, (2) having a proper purpose, and (3) having the expenditures communicated with simplicity.

Finally there are other areas in the school district that need to be closely monitored, as far as fiscal expenditures go, and ratios are a good tool to monitor those departments' activities.

Chapter 2

Looking at the Past to Predict the Future

The path to predicting student achievement through finance is taking past financial data and predicting future student performance. The discussion will begin with looking at budgets versus expenditures and understanding the distinct differences between the two.

This chapter presents how readily available financial data are used and tests if an initiative aimed at student achievement is working or being implemented with fidelity. It also discusses a couple of core concepts that have been proven to increase student achievement and how financial data are used to see if some of these strategies are being implemented.

The chapter closes with a look at a school-specific concern list and how financial data can help by providing more insight into that list.

BUDGET VERSUS EXPENDITURES

It is important to distinguish between the technical meaning and the often used meanings of the words "budget" and "expenditure." The word "budget" is often used to describe all of the districts purchases. In reality it is the plan of what the district is going to spend. A big difference between school districts and almost every other business entity is that school districts can be guaranteed to receive most of the money/revenue that is projected to be given to them.

That is why much emphasis is put on the budget because for the most part, all of the money is going to be received, thereby making the plan or budget a reality. Moreover, a significant amount of laws are tied to the budget because it is a way to control spending from the onset of the school year, and those controls need to be in place to ensure transparency for the tax payer.

In a for-profit business there may be shortfalls or a surplus in revenues, and all of those have to be accounted for in moving the budget up or down throughout the year, but the key for for-profit businesses is revenue and profit: the top and bottom line.

Whereas a school district, for the most part, is not in the business of making money, they are in the business of teaching and learning, and spending money to accomplish those goals. Therefore, the budget is viewed differently in school districts than it is for, say, a manufacturing company.

Expenditures refer to the actual money spent indicating what the district has actually expended its resources on as opposed to the plan the district has to expend its said resources on. That is why it is important to compare the budget versus the actual amount of money spent on a specific object or activity.

Furthermore, it is important to look at variances between actual expenditures and the budget—that is, what was spent versus what was planned to be spent, and investigate why such a variance occurred; these figures, budgeted amount, and expenditure amount for a specific category are usually on all school district internal financial reports.

It is important to run a budget as tight or close as possible because both sides, going over or under budget, can have an adverse effect on the performance or at least the efficiency of the district. For example, if not enough money is budgeted for critical operations (salaries, utilities, transportation, etc.), then other areas will be affected to make up the shortfall.

Those other areas usually involve professional development, supplies, and equipment—which are very important for student achievement. The key to remember is that school districts have a lot of fixed variable costs.

These costs are associated with activities the school district must do; transportation and child nutrition, to name a few, have to be procured (fixed costs); however, the cost is based on the number of children served (variable costs). It is critical that the budget is true for these costs because the money to fund these mandates will have to come from somewhere, and it is more efficient to control where the money comes from initially than trying to come up with the money at the last minute.

Think about a household budget; if there aren't enough funds allotted for the utility bills, and it is common knowledge that a household needs its utilities, then there will have to be a cut somewhere else. Discretionary spending will probably be on the chopping block. If the household consists of a couple, then that couple should have funds budgeted to go out to eat, to have a break from the day-to-day stressors of family and household life.

Going out to eat or on a date is beneficial in many ways; it can help the couple relax, strengthen their relationship, and foster quality time. With that said, not budgeting correctly can wreak havoc on a couple, because it will eat into their disposable income and, at least, partially eliminate their quality and relaxation time.

The same is true for school districts because the first items that will be cut if there is a shortfall are staff development programs, supplies, and hourly labor expenses that are critical to the day-to-day operations of a school district and ultimately student achievement.

If eliminating key ingredients to a highly functional household is the effect of poor budgeting on a household, imagine what it can do to a multimillion dollar organization.

On the flip side, if too much was budgeted, then there could be a scramble to spend money that should have a plan attached to it. A way to protect against scrambling and wasteful spending would be to have a wish list for any line items that may run a little loose at or toward the end of the year.

At the school level if a particular school has budgeted too much in a particular place, and the school is faced with a decision to either spend the money or lose it, the school will spend it. Since there has been a rush placed on spending the funds, there is a considerable chance that funds were not maximized.

The bottom line is to look at expenditure data when trying to make a firm decision when something is happening and use budgeted data to see if a plan is in place to make sure something is going to happen or to make a corrective action.

It is important to mention that when creating a budget, it is imperative to not only look at the budget from the previous year but also to look at the expenditure data from the previous three years to see if there is a trend. If the fiscal year is not over with yet, create projections to have an estimate in place for the expenditure data at the end of the year.

For example, if it is April 1 and the fiscal year ends on June 30 then 75 percent of the fiscal year had gone by. To predict out the expenditures, take the total amount of expenditures and divide it by the percentage of the year that has passed. The answer will give you the expected amount to be spent for the year.

HOW TO TEST IF AN INITIATIVE IS WORKING

If a one-to-one initiative is in place at a particular school, then it could be expected that expenditures on paper would drop. In this scenario it would be appropriate to pull expenditure data halfway through the school year to make sure that the expenditures on paper has decreased significantly year after year.

If the expenditure data was pulled and the expenditures on paper have not decreased, it could be derived that some teachers are still using worksheets and paper copies opposed to using digital content. Therefore, the initiative may have not taken hold with all teachers and the projected achievement gains will not be reached, if the gains were based on the implementation of technology.

This was simply derived by asking: What should a school save money on when implementing a one-to-one initiative? The answer is a reduction in paper, because most content will be delivered electronically.

When the school year begins, the budget for paper should be checked to make sure the amount was reduced; if the budgeted amount for paper is the same as the previous year, the school could be unknowingly hiding funds that could be spent elsewhere or they have no plans of implementing the initiative with fidelity.

This example of paper expenditures related to an investment in technology could be used on the district level if the district is one to one or even if they have made a significant investment in technology. It is important to think of all the ramifications that can happen when making investment decisions.

If there is a significant investment made to increase efficiency and lower costs, then those initiatives need to be monitored, not only for fidelity but also for return on investment. For example, if efficient heating and cooling units are installed in school buildings or if GPS units are installed in yellow buses, then there should be cost savings and the budget and expenditure data should mirror that savings.

To figure that out, the cost per pupil could be computed and compared year after year; remember that the cost per pupil is used to keep calculations relative, eliminating the natural variance for increase or decrease of students. Then if there is a reduction, there would be a freeing up of funds to use elsewhere.

CONCEPTS

A tool for making decisions is to use the data that is available and accurate. Some well-known and published factors that contribute to student achievement are as follows:

- Student visible learning
- Formative teacher evaluation
- Direct instruction
- Peer tutoring
- Classroom management
- Parental involvement
- Writing programs

- Computer-assisted instruction
- Class size

Financial data cannot relate to some of the above concepts. However, financial data can add insight into some of the concepts, augmenting a level of measurement to ensure integration, for example, computer-assisted instruction.

Financial data could be used to determine if computer-assisted instruction is being utilized to a certain extent. The process starts by looking up the expenditures on computers at the specific school in question.

To create a baseline, use five years of expenditures. Use inventory data to see if in the initial year enough computers were purchased for a one-to-one initiative; if not, then the cost should grow (partially due to inflation) year after year until the one-to-one initiative is achieved, because more and more computers need to be purchased every year, especially in and after the first year the refresh cycle starts.

As an additional step, look at the district's technology plan to know what the refresh rate should be in order to predict more accurately the year a steep increase in expense should occur due to the start of a new refresh cycle unless all the computers are purchases before the first refresh year.

If all the computers were purchased before the first refresh year, then the expenditure and budget should remain flat to the first year of the technology initiative plus inflation.

When looking at table 2.1, assume that this is a standard elementary school with 600 students and a computer costs $500; for a three-year plan, there would need to be an investment on average of $100,000 per year.

A goal for the district is to implement technology, through a one-to-one initiative, to help students become more comfortable with technology in an educational setting in three years. (There are many other facets to a goal like this, but for this example, it is important to not just focus on the goal itself but on how to use financial data to measure its implementation.)

A one-to-one school is defined by having technology for either take home or in-school use where it is a device per student at all times.

Table 2.1 Computer Expenses

Year	Description	Expenses
2010–2011	Computer hardware	$125,000
2011–2012	Computer hardware	$103,000
2012–2013	Computer hardware	$112,000
2013–2014	Computer hardware	$145,000
2014–2015	Computer hardware	$140,000
2015–2016	Computer hardware	$150,000*

*Budgeted amount

The question is if the district has a three-year refresh plan, did this school do what it needed to do to become a one-to-one school and follow district policy? The answer is yes and yes; they should have achieved one-to-one status about halfway through 2012–2013, and for the refresh plan, there would need to be an expense in 2013–2014 greater than the amount spent three years ago, and that is in fact the case. (The school spent $145,000, which is more than the $125,000 spent in 2010–2011.)

To bring this full circle, when looking at the necessity for computer-assisted instruction it could be said that this school is putting itself in a great position to offer that type of instruction. The key to this information is to look at the big picture of the district, which is usually called a "strategic plan." If the district has identified the need for computer-based instruction, this would be simple data to pull or request to have pulled. The critical information to see if the school is following the district's strategic plan can be listed as follows:

- Number of children
- Cost per machine
- District refresh rate
- Time available to achieve goal
- Expenditure data of the past five years

Once this data is compiled, a simple arithmetic can be performed to see if the school is doing what it needs to do.

The inventory data could be requested and desegregated to reach the same outcome as the above example, but each machine would need to be counted and the year it was purchased would also need to be captured to convey if the refresh plan was being implemented and to see if the computers were actually being purchased.

It is simpler to pull the expenditure data and reconcile it than to pull the inventory data to find if the school is on par.

This expenditure data could be pulled for all elementary schools in the district, and if there are letter grades assigned to the schools (table 2.2), have those grades and the data analyzed to see if there is any correlation between the expenditures on computers and the grade of the school. This concept of building correlation to see if a concept works has been presented before; however, the expenditure data is very rarely used.

As a side note, one complaint about this calculation might be that the computer prices are not standard and cannot easily be compared. A best practice could be to incorporate into the technology plan what would be a standard machine for elementary, secondary, career technical education, and so on.

This works for two reasons: one is simplicity and the other is it enables the technology department to become masters of the machines used in that

Table 2.2 School Grades Compared to Technology Expenditures

School	Elm St. Elem.	Main St. Elem.	North Elem.
School grade	A	C	D
Technology exp. ($)	115,000.00	65,000.00	37,500.00

district as opposed to being responsible for many different machines and not being efficient at any of them.

CONCERN LIST

Every high-ranking school district official should have an internal concern list for particular schools that are going to deviate from the norm, that is, a running list of schools that may not perform per the required standards. The deviation/standards can be in many facets: safety, academic performance, infrastructure performance, and so on. This concern list can be validated by looking at financial data. Below are several things that can be looked at for substantiation.

- Attendance data (substitute teacher cost)—Student engagement and instruction that is focused at the student are necessary for a school to succeed, and it takes a highly trained teacher to accomplish engagement and direct instruction. Usually that is outside the scope of a substitute teacher.
- Staff development expenditures—Collaboration is a key factor to moving a school forward; it is important that funds be spent on staff development. If not, then there is a good chance there is little collaboration going on, because nobody is learning anything new.
- Expenditures on parental involvement—Parental engagement is critical in school success; to engage parents, for the most part, there has to be some funds spent, either on food or on supplies for the meetings with parents.
- Technology expenditures—Measuring expenditures on not only actual hardware or machines but also on software, such as reading, math, and writing programs.
- District-wide and school-specific per pupil expenditure data on instructional and student support services (listed separately)—Is this school on the concern list receiving more than other schools? If it is on a concern list, then it would be proactive to steer resources to those respective schools. Furthermore, a reason the particular school is on the concern list can be because of a downward trend in resources distributed. It is especially important to review student services expenditure data because low-performing schools have tendencies to be those with a high at-risk population and that population needs the more than average attention from student services.

It is imperative to meet frequently at the district level about the performance of particular schools early in the school year. Furthermore, it is important to work on the progress of schools that are not performing well. Several states assign letter grades to individual schools on a statewide universal scale. Some education officials, at many of the states, argue that the grades are too stringent.

Regardless of the stringency, it is a metric that the officials can use to pinpoint which schools need extra attention initially. Also those school grades and expenditure data can be compared on both ends of the spectrum. Schools that perform well can also have their data examined and best practices can be established.

SUMMARY

This chapter started out with giving clarity between budgets and expenditures and looking at the necessity of having budgets on par with actual expenditures. The chapter moved on to looking at initiatives and how to use financial data to test an initiative's effectiveness. Then an introduction of core concepts that could act as a catalyst to student achievement and how some of the concepts can be gauged with financial data were provided. Finally the notion of having a concern list for schools that may not be performing well and how financial data can help validate that list and give insight on how to correct the path of those schools were discussed.

Chapter 3

How to Use District Efficiency Indicators

To get a full picture of the district's financial health, the district should use district efficiency indicators and learn how to analyze and present the indicators through ratios and trend lines. This chapter discusses different departments of the school district and how to include them in the district's analysis even if those departments do not directly affect teaching and learning. The chapter wraps up with a sample data card looking at sample data and trend lines.

WHAT IS DISTRICT EFFICIENCY?

It is important to reiterate the notion that a district has to incur many costs for its day-to-day operations that do not contribute directly to teaching and learning. At the onset, these expenses may not directly affect student achievement, but they do cost money.

If these costs run over or consume too much of the budget, then they will creep into the areas that directly affect student achievement, and they need to be monitored because they are critical to teaching and learning.

Examples of these costs are as follows:

- Transportation—The cost to transport students to and from school.
- Child nutrition—The cost to provide, at the minimum, lunch for students of the districts. Other meals can be provided at the districts' discretion.
- Maintenance—The cost of upkeep and cleaning of the buildings used in educating the children of the district.

- Technology—The cost of student-related technology purchases and the cost of the district's infrastructure to support the technology. For example, the actual cost of the internet and/or the email service provided to students.

Some may argue that technology is not a requirement to run a district's day-to-day operations, but for this book it is. Whether it is for the infrastructure of the district or for student learning, technology is critical in moving a district forward.

Many times district officials and school boards have an expectation that there is money that is untapped or just lying around in a filing cabinet somewhere. In reality the money is not lying around per se, it is being spent on the things that do not align to the district's vision and mission.

If the above operations are monitored and benchmarked externally against other districts and/or against previous year's performance, then perhaps there is some new money, like a pot of gold at the end of the rainbow; the caveat here is that most of the time the rainbow needs to be created.

Children from poverty-stricken families are more likely to encounter literacy problems throughout their educational career. One root factor, apart from the numerous environmental (single-parent homes, generational poverty, or lack of educational resources in the home) factors, is the word count such children possess or lack thereof. This can be identified in Pre-K or kindergarten at the earliest.

This lack of word count has a potential for a downward spiral, because if that gap is not closed, then discipline issues will arise because the child will not understand what is happening in class and will act out from boredom or embarrassment.

A district that is high in poverty identifies this trend and realizes that there are processes it can put in place to help close the word count gap. However, this process costs money—substantial amounts of money. Where would this district, which matches many districts in America, find the money—its pot of gold—to implement this process?

An excellent place to start would be to look at the operations listed above and begin to reconcile the expenditures to see if there is any slack in the budget or if there are operations that lead to wasteful spending.

For example, a district's child nutrition department may operate in the red or negative, forcing the district to contribute funds from other sources to maintain the child nutrition department, which is a necessity to the district. To combat this rescue mission for child nutrition, this district would start by looking at previous years' data to check if the department was ever profitable.

If the department did have a profitable past, then it is necessary to go back in time and look at what the department did differently in the past. It could be a matter of a rise in food prices and not a relative rise in prices charged to the students. If the department has not been profitable, then it is time to look outside the district and enquire about a neighboring profitable district's financial records, as long as the district has a similar demographic as to compare apples to apples.

Once the difference, albeit internally or benchmarking, is established, then the district could make the appropriate changes and forecast the cost savings (money from more efficient operations—filling the pot of gold). If the labor costs are higher than normal, then through attrition, a new pay scale can be created and implemented without affecting the currently employed staff. (This is a slower process for a smaller district or one that has lower turnover.)

Once the new process is done, the cost savings can be diverted to a literacy program to help close the word count gap and eventually help lower discipline issues and raise test scores.

Child nutrition is a different animal because it is set up to run as a for-profit business, and the district inherently knows, unlike in the case of other departments, such as transportation, at the end of the year if the department is losing money.

One factor would be: Does the department routinely run over budget? If so, in what areas? Sticking with transportation, is the fuel budget constantly violated? Perhaps the budget has not been adjusted properly for inflation or the routes are not being run as accurate as before or as they need to be.

If there is no initial inkling that the department is running efficiently, take a two-pronged approach. First, look at past data and make it relative, cost per student. Second, benchmark other districts in the same relative manner, per student. This approach will help ensure efficiency.

RATIOS

Ratios are an elegant and simplistic way to look at expenditure data. They can be used to compare expenditures from multiple platforms. Budgets for school districts can range from millions to billions of dollars.

There might be a time when two districts may have similar demographics, but the budgets are not similar and therefore not comparable. This becomes an issue when trying to benchmark one district against another.

For example, there may be a district that has 10,000 students and is 65 percent African American, 30 percent Caucasian, and 5 percent Native American. Then there is a district in the same state that has 3,000 students with almost the exact same demographics. The first district with 10,000 children may have a budget that is over three times the size of the district that has 3,000 students.

With that said, it would be inappropriate to look at actual dollars spent on a specific purpose. However, it would be appropriate to look at ratios. For example, how much did the districts spend per pupil on technology?

Finally, ratios, because of their elegance and simplicity, can be applicable when comparing schools also; similarly, the demographics may be the same, but the budgets are not.

Ratios may be especially useful when looking across state lines. Some states pay less in salaries than other states. When comparing actual dollars spent, the states with the larger salaries are going to have more dollars allocated and usually spent in their budget, for the most part, even if the number of teachers is exactly the same as states with smaller average teacher salaries.

Therefore, to say whether one state spent more on teachers than another may, based on pure dollars spent, be an accurate statement; it tells us nothing about what is important, which is how many teachers relative to the number of students that state made possible through its allotment to K–12 education when compared to another state.

Think of it like the cost of living in different areas of the United States. A 2,400-square-foot house may cost half a million dollars in some parts of California. If that same house is in rural North Dakota, it may only cost 180K. Same house, way different price tags.

Examples of the practical use of ratios is looking at larger picture objectives; since the essence of ratios is to easily compare things, it is easier to compare larger picture objectives to see if further investigation is required.

No need to do more work or waste time if things are running efficiently. Ratios work well when wanting to compare the percentage of certain items or categories to entire amount of expenditures. For example, how much money is spent on instructional salaries compared to the total amount of expenditures on salaries?

Ratios are extremely useful when benchmarking districts versus districts and schools versus schools. An illustrated example of a ratio is how much funds a school district spends on transportation compared to another district from the same state. District A has a total budget of $100,000,000 and District B has a total budget of $65,000,000.

District A has a size of 120 square miles and District B has 75 square miles. District A has 20,000 students, whereas District B has 8,500 students. District A has transportation costs of $3,000,000 on its audit financial statements and District B has $1,200,000.

Table 3.1 has a plethora of data. Looking at the ratios, the two districts ran very tight on their budgets and that is a good thing because there was no slack in the budget that could be used in other places such as curriculum and instruction. District B is more efficient than District A when looking at the percentage of total expenditures.

Table 3.1 Transportation Analysis

	District A	District B
Total budget	$100,000,000	$65,000,000
Total expenditures	$99,000,000	$63,000,000
Square miles	120	75
Number of students	20,000	8,500
Transportation costs	$3,000,000	$1,200,000
Ratios		
Trans. cost % of total budget	3.00%	1.85%
Trans. cost of total expenditures	3.03%	1.90%
Trans. cost per sq. mile	$25,000	$16,000
Cost per student	$150.00	$141.18

However, when looking at cost per pupil, the two districts are not that far apart—only about $9 or 6 percent. How could this be? The answer lies within the other ratio the cost per square mile, there is a 32 percent difference between Districts A and B or District A spends 32 percent more per square mile than District B. A very simple answer to this example could be what is known as "corner stops."

Corner stops are where a school bus stops at common points to several houses as opposed to each house individually. If this is not the answer, the answer would lie in the distance the bus travels as opposed to possible higher labor or parts cost. District B could use corner stops where District A may not.

On a purely financial basis corner stops seem more fiscally appropriate than stopping at every house. It is important to see how ratios make this type of analysis quick and simple once the data is compiled, and for the source of the data, audit financial statement, it can be deemed as very accurate.

OTHER AREAS TO CONSIDER

There are other departments that are necessary to run the operations of a district that may not be related to the student directly. Examples of these departments are as follows:

- Finance—Processes payroll (paying of the employees), purchasing, and accounts payable (paying the vendors)
- Human resources—Hiring, evaluating, compensation, and firing of the school districts employee; benefits may also be housed here or in finance
- Federal programs—Ensure implementation and compliance of programs set forth by the federal government

Examples of other departments, usually outside the school building, related to students but still need to be monitored are as follows:

- Testing—The hub for the districts testing needs and execution
- Student services—Guidance, social work, nurses, sometimes physical education, and dropout prevention
- Exceptional children—Any services that need to be offered to a child that has been deemed exceptional
- Curriculum and instruction—The center for all teaching and learning in the district

These programs do play a critical role in student achievement. The costs can be monitored, on a per-pupil basis, for spikes and opportunity. However, there may be federal or state mandates attached to these departments that require an uptick in spending.

Those mandates need to be tracked and communicated to stakeholders because if there is not revenue to match the uptick in cost, then those mandates should be considered unfunded.

As a brief side note, unfunded mandates are like the auxiliary departments listed above. If they are not checked, they will creep into other areas of the district and take away spending power that could contribute directly to student achievement. Therefore, any elected body of stakeholders is in critical need of the unfunded mandates because it could be a rallying cry for more funds.

It is important to not leave a department untouched when it comes to maximization testing. There is potential for savings all over the district. To benchmark these other departments against other districts may be difficult as a whole. For example, a district may include nurses in another category opposed to student services.

When comparing percentage of the budget spent on the finance department, it is important to see what is included in its portfolio of services. For example, the department that handles the employee's benefits can sometimes fall under finance's umbrella. If District A has the benefits department in its portfolio of services offered by finance and District B does not, it would not be accurate to compare the amount spent relative to the total budget for each district's respective finance department.

To eliminate the same confusion when comparing other items in the school districts, be very specific when benchmarking or know what goes into the cost data to safeguard from any unnecessary variances—for example, only comparing nursing costs against nursing costs as opposed to comparing both student services budgets.

However, if comparing internally year after year, it is fine to compare the entire department because its structure has probably not changed.

Description	TREND	13-14	14-15	15-16 proj.
Transportation		$ 342	$ 381	$ 256
Operation Of Plant		$ 417	$ 473	$ 550
Technology		$ 273	$ 228	$ 215
CN		$ 579	$ 630	$ 487
Central Office		$ 482	$ 357	$ 385
Instructional Support		$ 421	$ 368	$ 283
Noninstructional Support		$ 387	$ 414	$ 355
Certified Teachers		$ 2,954	$ 3,124	$ 3,035
Teacher Assistants		$ 310	$ 355	$ 357
Office Support		$ 295	$ 291	$ 259
Technician		$ 50	$ 54	$ 48
Salaries		$ 5,804	$ 6,099	$ 5,662
Employer Provided Ben.		$ 1,970	$ 2,032	$ 2,017
Purchased Services		$ 974	$ 1,002	$ 1,071
Supplies and Materials		$ 784	$ 647	$ 542

Figure 3.1 Efficiency Indicators

Be careful of years with leadership changes because that may signal a change at the district level of what expenditures are tied to what departments, due to personal preferences of the new leadership. If there are significant changes and if they are not factored in, it would lead to a cloudy or inaccurate analysis.

PRESENTATION OF THE INDICATORS

When presenting data simplicity is key! Please see the below sample of what a district cost report may look like.

The above data card was created by taking the expenditure data from the respective category for the year referenced at the top of the corresponding column and divided by the number of students that were enrolled, on average, for the respective school year.

By looking at the trend line for each category, it is easily understandable as to which way the cost per pupil is heading. Any category that is going up would require a more in-depth look at the expenditures. On the other hand, looking at certified teachers the respective trend line shows that expense is going down. The initial thought is that the district is saving money on certified teachers, which seems like a good thing. However, it needs to be said that salaries should always rise because of, at the minimum, a yearly cost of living adjustment.

With the trend lines in figure 3.1 showing a decrease, it would mean that the teachers have less experience than they did the previous year or there are more un-certified teachers teaching, perhaps substitute teachers in vacant positions. This drop would warrant a deeper look into working conditions, turnover data, and vacancies—all that from a little line. That trend line is a powerful piece to the message that the financial data is trying to communicate.

SUMMARY

This chapter looked at district efficiency and introduced the idea that a district can find money to fund other projects by looking within its own current expenditures. It is especially important to look at operations or departments the district has to have for its day-to-day operations. Ratios are very simple and useful; they help take down the barriers of difficulty in comparing data. Finally, presentation is the key because having financial data communicated through a trend line can send a powerful message.

Chapter 4

What Expenses to Include in the Indicators

How to determine what data is relevant and how to decipher through the data to truly only focus on what matters is one of the initial steps to honing in on student achievement. Next is the discussion on who needs the data so that the presentation of information can be useful and informative to the end user. The next question is: Why is financial data important? This chapter then wraps up with looking at financial data to predict student achievement and using district efficiency indicators to make sure all funds are being spent as efficiently as possible.

WHAT DATA IS RELEVANT?

Each school district is different; it is important to have a firm grasp of what the school district is composed of from a student perspective, creating a picture of the combinations of ethnicities, income, and performance levels. With this picture, the task of figuring out what really matters can take place.

For example, if there is an increase in English as a Second Language (ESL) students, that population may need additional ESL teachers and supplies to keep up with the growth. Is the increase in ESL spending relative to the total expenditure the same as the increased percentage of ESL students relative to the primarily English-speaking students?

The above example is to illustrate the need to focus on what is being measured. Therefore, measuring expenditures that directly affect academically gifted students will have no insight on the fostering of the increase of ESL students.

This comes full circle with the notion that, even though, some of the academically gifted students may be ESL students measuring the funding for the academically gifted students has no direct effect on funding the growth of ESL students. Only the funds spent directly on ESL students has that impact (to foster growth) and, therefore, should be the only number to be looked at.

Once again, with the above example, it is important to notice that financial data must match the criteria for which the analysis is taking place. If it is not relevant, it is useless for that particular scenario. If a car is overheating, the air in the tires is not the first thing that needs be checked. The radiator is the first thing that needs to be checked because the radiator plays a key role in preventing overheating in the vehicle.

Furthermore, it is important to know the solution for the problem. This may seem straightforward, but it is imperative to realize that analyzing the financial data is only the beginning; it will only determine if things are being done correctly initially or if there are downward trends ahead. The solution comes with the reallocation of funds, which is determined by analyzing the past financial data.

If there is a problem with out-of-school suspensions, pulling the financial statements will not help solve that problem; the financial statements will not even shed light on the problem of out-of-school suspensions.

However, if it is deemed that the suspension problem is due to environmental problems (poverty, non-stable home life, etc.), what are those environmental problems? Once those problems are ferreted out, then the financial statements can be pulled to see if any financial resources are being funneled to that area.

For example, if poverty is identified as an environmental factor. Has staff development program funds been spent to give poverty training or have materials been purchased to help eliminate the effect poverty has on students.

If there is no money being spent on the environmental problems due to lack of funds, then how can the district become more efficient in creating additional funds to help solve this out-of-school suspension problem?

Usually a district's strategic plan can lay out goals and add insight to where some potential opportunities may lie. For example, if a strategic plan identifies the need to increase the graduation rate, then the next question should be what are the things that can be implemented to increase the graduation rate? Then, do these things cost money or is there another way to implement them?

Therefore, it is important to know very specifically what items need to be solved or that contribute to the opportunity that is trying to be solved. Without the specific information, it is like the district is spending money for the sake of it because that is what school districts do. Whereas there needs to be data-driven decisions made and the data is the financial data.

WHO NEEDS THE DATA?

Understanding the end user is just as important knowing the problem at hand or the outcome that is being predicted. Simplicity, being a necessity for any means of communication, is a must for financial data; therefore, regardless of the end user, the data should be easy to understand.

It is important to go a step further because a person may not know that they need financial data to make decisions or predict outcomes. Therefore, there needs to be a standard reporting process for the district so that any red flags are always out in front. Also, a staff member may have experience gained in other districts or industries which may help them see a number or ratio and know that the number or ratio may inherently be too high or low.

Bottom line is to make the relationship between the finance department and the rest of the district as cohesive as possible. It is important that the person communicating the financial data to predict student achievement knows who the end user is for the particular data. For example, the human resources department should be more focused on staff retention/turnover costs, opposed to cost per meal for every student in the first through third grade. Therefore, the presenter of the financial data needs to be astute to the person receiving the message.

With that said and knowing that people generally have short attention spans, and financial data can be dry, it is imperative that the person on the other end of the communication can relate to the data which will lead to engagement between the presenter and the recipient of the financial data.

WHY IS THE DATA IMPORTANT?

Data are important to make decisions and especially important is past financial data. When looking at any data, future trends are, like the weather, difficult to predict. However, it is important to have some idea of what the future may look like, because as the old saying goes: failing to plan is planning to fail.

Therefore, future forecast and projection data are important, for example, things like student enrollment and funding amounts. In addition, taking into account multiyear expenditures may help student achievement but reduce flexibility by tying up a large amount of funding—think of a large multiyear lease payment on a large piece of capital equipment.

Keeping with the idea of having two functions of finance data, namely efficiency indicators and predicting student achievement, it is important to look at each set and then drill down to look at the specifics of each set, because each set of data tells a different story.

PREDICTING STUDENT ACHIEVEMENT

Looking at the expenditures that predict student achievement, it is important to break the expenditure data down even further. For example, costs related to substitute teachers. Please remember that if substitute teacher costs have risen year over year, it is important to look at the specific situations because that could be a sign of high vacancies.

However, is the increase in sub-costs due to an increase in staff development program on days where students are scheduled to attend class? Furthermore, if this is the case, the budget codes used to code the absences should tell what type of absences they are; it should be relatively easy to compare the amount spent on general absences and/or district or school initiatives (staff development program).

What this means is that there could be a positive correlation for the uptick in sub-costs or it could be a negative correlation. The positive is if indeed there is a staff development program going on—it could lead to collaboration. Whereas the negative piece is an increase in absences.

There could be an agreement either way about staff development programs on days when students are in class, but for this example, it is important to illustrate that a negative (increase in substitute costs) could be a positive (more teachers participating in staff development programs).

The core of the idea of using financial data to predict student achievement is the necessity to drill down to the detail of the expenditure. Sticking with the substitute teacher cost, digging down into the data to look for the creation of the purchase is critical. For further understanding of the predicative nature of the specific transaction, it is necessary to realize the cause of the expenditure to begin with.

Why was the money spent on a substitute teacher? If the answer to the question is to cover absences, then that data should trigger the necessary reaction. For example, if the expenditure is for an absence, then it should be second nature that an absence needs to be addressed because it equals a lack of consistency in the classroom.

Furthermore, a lack of consistency in the classroom leads to lower performance among certain groups of children (at-risk), then the financial data just predicted that those students will perform less than expected due to a decrease in consistency.

It is important to understand the demographic of the district. The demographic will help to determine what deserves the most attention for measurement. In other words, a budget friendly hotel is not going to be concerned with the thread count of their sheets, nor should a district that is mostly affluent worry about feeding all children for free, even though for some children it would be beneficial but not for all.

Furthermore, there are universal metrics that all districts can use: measuring parental involvement, substitute cost data, student support information, monitoring technology implementation, and rewarding success.

DISTRICT EFFICIENCY INDICATORS

Along the same lines as predicting student achievement, it is important to look at individual costs. District efficiency is the key to finding existing money with the district's current budget to fund new initiatives. For example, transportation; if the cost per pupil has risen year after year, which part of the individual cost per pupil has risen? Therefore, the transportation analysis needs to be broken down by, but not limited to:

- Fuel—If fuel costs have risen and the total number of miles has stayed relatively flat, then it is important to see if the actual cost of fuel has risen or if there is a lot of idle time out there (where the bus is turned on but not moving).
- Driver payroll—If the cost for bus driver pay increased but the number of students or miles driven stayed flat, there could be time creep where the driver is parking somewhere off the route and just riding the clock, or he may be clocking in and going to socialize or ride the clock somewhere besides the bus.
- Clerical—This looks at the amount per pupil spent on administrative salaries; this measurement is critical for districts where the number of children is shrinking because the number of clerical personnel may need to be reduced through attrition.
- Parts (including tires)—The opportunity with parts may lie within an efficient inventory system that prevents theft. If there is a spike in this portion of the cost, theft may be a primary reason. Look at tires especially because they become the low-hanging fruit for theft.

Maintenance analysis also has many different facets. With many different facets comes many measurement tools and opportunities. The facets can be broken down to, but not limited to:

- Parts—With parts it is important to not only look at theft, as in transportation, but also if the district is spending money on the same type of parts for the same machinery and/or equipment. If so, there may be a larger and ultimately less expensive, in the long term, alternative to the current way the machinery/equipment is being fixed.

- Labor—What is the cost per pupil of each maintenance worker and how has that looked over time? There are two things that can help even further with this measurement. One is to break down each maintenance worker into their appropriate subset—that is, plumber, HVAC technician, painter, or general laborer (there may be more subsets)—and look at the cost of each subset on a per-pupil basis. Second, is there a management system for work orders? If so, is there a correlation between the amount spent per pupil in the subsets that increased, if there is an increase, and the amount of work orders? Is it vice versa where there is a reduction in cost and work orders? If there is a reduction on both sides, cost per pupil and work orders, then there may be an opportunity to benchmark what that particular subset has done. They may have introduced new technology to the subset that lowered costs over time or other best practices.
- Utilities—This a huge place for potential savings; there is a variety of things that can be done to lower utility expenses—behavioral changes and performance contracting, to name a few. However, if those two things, namely behavioral changes and performance contracting, are done through a company, then the savings are usually purely cost avoidance, or the utilities bills stay the same over time, meaning the district saves the amount of inflation. For the purpose of this text, look at the utility spend year after year, and if there is a sharp increase (greater than 2 percent) look at the amount consumed, whether it is water, electricity, or natural gas. If the amounts are not relative, then there is a usage problem and a behavioral change can be made; in other words, force people to turn out lights, computers, and smart boards when they leave. Furthermore, look at utility expense on a building-by-building basis per pupil. It would be cumbersome to look at it purely from a district standpoint because the ages of the buildings, which affects consumption, fluctuates too much in a school district.
- Contracted services—This part can be a vast array of items, from outsourcing mowing and fire extinguisher maintenance to changing air filters. It basically covers anything that has been outsourced. As a side note, it is always good to look at the contracts and compare competition or put out bids to see if there is a less expensive option out there. A telling sign of needing an investigation would be a spike on the amount spent perpupil. However, the number of buildings also needs to be considered. If the district is going through a heavy growth spurt with significant amount of new school construction, expect that the expense per pupil will grow, because there will be more of whatever is being serviced out there due to more buildings/campuses, but do not forget that there may be a threshold where it is less expensive to hire someone than to outsource.
- Clerical—This is the amount spent on any type of office support staff. Not only is this useful to look for large variances, especially upward, but to

benchmark against other districts to see if there are more efficient ways to have the office support staff operate.

Child nutrition or the operations of the districts cafeterias is one of the only for-profit entities in the school district. Therefore, it is imperative to run this operation as efficiently as possible. Even though the profits may be limited or restricted to the child nutrition department, the department can pay for its worker's compensation insurance along with indirect cost back to the district if that is applicable state-wide.

It would be appropriate to think of each school as its own restaurant. Restaurants measure some of the same ratios that should be monitored in a school cafeteria. There are three main components to monitor in child nutrition:

- Food cost—Food should be the biggest expenditure of the child nutrition department. It is important to watch the food cost as a percentage of sales (a common managerial accounting method for a for-profit entity) as a driver of price. In other words if food cost rises to 45 percent and the budgets were built on a 40 percent cost, then it is time to raise prices to bring it down to the budgeted 40 percent. An increased food cost can come from one of two places: waste (too much food is prepared and then the extras are thrown or given away) or a rise in the actual food cost and not a rise in the price charged.
- Labor cost—It is important to look at this and set a threshold that cannot be crossed; a large amount of child nutrition workers are paid hourly and their hours can be adjusted to reflect the level of demand. Therefore, this is the easiest metric to fix because as opposed to having to lay people off or working through attrition, the hours the employees work can be cut. There may be some states where there are union parameters; if that is true, then attrition will be the next option.
- Supplies—There is a substantial amount of consumables used in the child nutrition department, and it is important they are monitored because they could be a major drain on the financial performance of the overall program. Looking at this pupil will suffice.

Finally, capital equipment purchases should be monitored and presented in a schedule with the appropriate budgeting included; for example, if next year it is known that 40K ovens will need to be purchased, the budget, for the appropriate year, should reflect that, to either have a constant place for capital expenditures in the budget or a plan in place. If this is an unusual expense, the department can save the money the year before and then budget the funds, in the appropriate/next year with the said savings or fund balance, from the previous year(s), to cover the expenditures in the appropriate year.

If a person knows he or she is going to need a new car within the next year, he or she may cut back on going out to eat to save money for a down payment for that said new car. Another scenario is that he or she may constantly pay more on their current car note if he or she knows that he or she likes a new car every two years and that additional payment will help him or her from being upside down when he or she goes to purchase a new car. In either scenario there is a plan in place for the large expenditure.

SUMMARY

Knowing who, what, and why, and using that information to form a depiction of the end user of the financial data is critical because that depiction will provide the road map to ensure student performance. If the who, what, and why elements are not considered, then the data becomes ambiguous and almost useless because it has no point to it outside of the finance office.

There are several elements that can be looked at for student achievement. The lynchpin is to know what is proven to ensure student achievement and figure out how to use money to implement that process or accomplish that goal. Finally there are many areas in the district where there may be an opportunity to save money. It is critical to leave no stone unturned when the need arises for additional funding to increase student achievement. If a new plan is identified and additional funding is needed, then funding may be available within current operations.

Chapter 5

Child Nutrition Ratios

It is important to look at child nutrition (CN) and to make sure the program is profitable and that it relates to student achievement. The first section of this chapter discusses about the importance of CN and student achievement, how to get everyone fed, and ways to make money.

The second section discusses the intangibles that go into a successful CN department. The third and final section looks at the cost structures of the CN department, and how to use those structures to desegregate through that cost information to make great decisions.

THE GOALS OF CN

The function of CN has two big picture objectives. The first objective is to get everyone fed. The simplest way to understand this is that a hungry child is one who, even though wants to learn, is unable to overcome the hunger and consequently has more difficult time learning than his or her peers who are not hungry.

There is distinct research that links a decrease in hunger to an increase in achievement. With all that said, it is plain to see that student achievement is directly linked to the CN department.

It is important to realize what it truly means to get everyone fed. Some school districts have the community eligibility program (CEP), which provides federal funding for all students who participate. In other words, breakfast and lunch are free to all students at eligible schools.

CEP is the easiest way to solve the riddle of getting everyone fed in an economical manner. What if the district is not eligible for CEP or if they are in a state that does not have CEP? How does CN get everyone fed? The first place to start is to define what is meant by everyone and what is meant by fed.

Starting with everyone, to keep it simple, every child who does not bring food from home should be considered. A key metric in CN is participation, which looks at the percentage of children who participate by eating meals served by the CN department.

A reason that participation could be low can be from numerous reasons: the presentation of the food, the food offerings (a lot of restrictions are placed on the CN department and the general public does not understand these restrictions due to a lack of communication), a lack of alignment between menu offerings and family values (a family may want a child to consume soy milk and not cow's milk), price of the meals offered, the safety of the cafeteria, and the availability of certain menu items at certain times (every once in a while, a cafeteria may run out of a certain item at the last lunch period, and that item may be the only thing the child would like to eat).

Therefore, to say that the goal is to get everyone fed, and the reasons why the goal is not accomplished now is the place to start. For example, if participation is low, then a survey should be given to the school staff and students to find what are the areas of improvement and/or have senior leadership eat in the cafeterias; therefore, they can see for themselves where there is an opportunity.

To even go a step further, have outside staff members take 30–45 minutes a day to serve food and see for themselves the actual behind-the-scene operations and how the final product looks as it goes out to students.

If the choice is a survey, be sure to compose detailed questions on each of the objectives. An objective may be price, taste, or presentation. Also, it might not hurt to rank the objectives; there might be an opportunity to question certain objectives on multiple grounds, but do so only if the objective is head and shoulders above the rest. It is key to keep the survey short, so it will have a higher number of participants.

The second function is to make money and contribute some of those profits back to the district to help with other educational objectives. Also, it important to have nice facilities and the cafeteria can sometimes be a public place of meeting, especially for community schools. If the CN department is profitable, they can contribute to the construction and upkeep of the cafeteria facilities.

However, a balance must be maintained between the profitability and performance of the CN department. It is easy to go above and beyond in CN and spend a lot of money and not generate a lot of revenue.

It can be viewed that there are diminishing returns after a certain amount of resources is invested in CN. Labor costs is an appropriate place to look because there is less of an impact on students as opposed to spending a lot of money on food, which goes straight to the students and helps satisfy hunger, leading to higher achievement, as long as there is no wastage. Whereas there is arguably no direct correlation between labor hours and student achievement. Remember it is about getting the biggest bang for the buck.

Shrewd business decisions need to be made to make sure that the overall business of feeding children is profitable. It continues to be an opportunity for untapped funds for the district and the way to unleash those funds is to make shrewd and profitable decisions.

CAFETERIAS AND COUNTRY CLUBS

Cafeterias and country clubs should have a lot in common. Country clubs make it a passion to cater to their members, try to make the club feel like a second home to its members, and to maximize profits, so that they do not have to assess their members to cover their loses. Imagine if the cafeterias were run in the same manner as country clubs; it almost seems crazy.

However, it is not crazy because if a cafeteria is dirty and not visually appealing that is potential profit going down the drain.

The wonderful thing about cafeterias is that a school district is allowed to make money off of them. Therefore, if a district is losing money from the CN operation, it is a travesty. Going back to the cafeteria and country club example, if a cafeteria looks inviting, offers some amenities, has products at a price that works for the consumer, and provides food that tastes good, it magically has a lot in common with a country club.

This example has nothing to do with numbers, but it is important to discuss because the CN can be a money maker—it just has to be visually pleasing to get started on the right foot. Imagine going into a restaurant and the staff was mean and the dining area is dirty and not pleasant to look at. That restaurant would probably have a tough time, like the cafeterias do sometimes, giving away even free meals.

Signage and communication help students make quick decisions. If a student is faced with many decisions, then he or she might lean to making no decision, which is making a decision not to spend money. The main catalyst behind this is the lack of time. Lunch time at a school can be very short because it is competing with instructional time. Also, there are a lot of other competing stimuli within the cafeteria: friends and other social interactions.

An example of amenities may be charging stations and café-style seating. Not to sound clichéd but these make the cafeteria a cool or hip place to be and that starts with inviting décor and food. A cafeteria can be a huge sense of pride for a student body; coincidentally, if a student body is proud to be in a cafeteria and inherently congregates there, it is a strong possibility they will spend money there.

This section should not be confused with trying to exploit children to spend money or to alienate children who cannot afford student lunch. As a child gets older, it becomes more aware of being labeled for free and reduced lunch; therefore, as the grade number increases, the level of participation decreases—which translates into less revenue.

It goes without saying that the transaction of a free or reduced lunch can be less evasive, so that the student does not become embarrassed and can freely participate in the free and reduced-lunch process.

Another issue is delinquent accounts. It becomes a rush to collect the funds before prom or graduation. With that said, there should be checkpoints throughout the year that try to true up the balances. Please check with local counsel first. For high schools have periodic times where, if the amount owed grows to over, say, $25, then a parking pass will be revoked.

It is important to look at things that are not curriculum specific but are a bonus to the students; these things should be ransomed for clearing up of delinquent accounts. A common practice is to give a student with a delinquent account a different meal and too many times that has brought negative publicity; therefore, it is more productive to be proactive and look at activities that the students like, where they would be motivated to pay off the debts, so that they may be able to participate in those said activities.

It cannot be emphasized enough that if the free and reduced-lunch process is student-friendly and not evasive, then chances are high that the delinquent accounts will shrink before the charges are incurred because those students that do not have the funds, who have the delinquent accounts, will use the tools they are allowed to use and perhaps participate in the free and reduced-lunch process.

LOOKING AT THE NUMBERS

Two financial statements have been presented below; the first one represents what will be found in the actual financial statements (figure 5.1), whereas the second one is a report that can be generated internally to create a holistic approach to evaluating the numbers, especially if the program is not profitable. Think of each statement as an outfit; the first statement, which is the official statement, is an outfit that would be worn in public, if going to, say, the movies, whereas the second statement is an outfit that would be worn around the house to watch a rental/streaming movie.

Both outfits serve the same purpose, but one is more appropriate for the public situation. Much like the statements, the outfit that is worn around the house can serve many purposes and is actually more useful than the outfit that is worn in public.

Operating revenues:	
Food sales	252,184
Operating expenses:	
Food cost:	
Purchase of food	1,163,000
Donated commodities	241,764
Salaries and benefits	1,855,103
Indirect costs	228,149
Materials and supplies	120,171
Repairs and maintenance	33,823
Depreciation	57,573
Non-capitalized equipment	377
Contracted services	6,355
Other	24,544
Total operating expenses	3,730,859
Operating loss	-3,478,675
Nonoperating revenues:	
Federal reimbursements	3,369,955
Federal commodities	241,764
Interest earned	2,245
Other	3,368
Total nonoperating revenues	3,617,332
Income before transfers	138,657
Transfers from other funds	45,001
Change in net position	183,658
Net position, beginning of year, as previously reported	1,280,765
Restatement	-412,928
Net position, beginning of year, as restated	867,837
Net position, end of year	1,051,495

Figure 5.1 Child Nutrition Revenues and Expenses

However, it is not appropriate due to social standards to wear the second outfit in public and the internal/second report is not officially appropriate to the reporting bodies that look at the financial statements for validity.

Analysis of the above statement can be broken down into a multistep process. The first step would be to change the numbers in this statement to per-pupil numbers, and the only thing needed to do that is the number of pupils for the appropriate reporting period.

Divide the number in question by the number of pupils to get the per-pupil number; for example, if the district from the above example had 6,000 pupils, then for the food sales figure it would be 252,184/6,000 = 42.03.

This means that there was $42.03 spent per pupil for the entire year on food. This statement is from a district that is 100 percent CEP. That majority of the revenues is listed in the nonoperating revenue section.

The next step is to a two-part process; if the department is losing money, then find a district that is making money and do step 1 for that district and compare the per-pupil numbers. Once the differences are found, dig deeper to see where the variances actually came from. To confirm the department is profitable, look at the income before transfers and subtract the depreciation number, because depreciation is a noncash expense.

If that number is positive, then the department should be profitable for the reporting period of the financial statements. Part 2 to step 2 is if the district has been profitable, create a multiyear comparison, by using previous years' financial statements and doing step 1 for the previous four years to see if there are any areas for improvement.

The spreadsheet on the next page (figure 5.2) is an internally generated report that will look at the figures in depth and over multiple years. It helps to give a different perspective to the data while making it more helpful for decision-making purposes.

It is important to look at the profitability of the program first; if the program is profitable, is the profit going up or down? How long has the department been profitable? If the department is not profitable, then it will take an in-depth investigation, like a detective looking, for clues at a crime scene. The classic saying, the devil is in the details, really applies here. The possible cause of the devil will be described in detail later.

If the department is profitable, it is important to look at the trend of profitability. If the profitability is shrinking per pupil, then the program should be treated as if it is losing money because it will soon be. In the next several paragraphs it is important to realize the lens that this data is being presented in: as a department that is losing money or the profitability is shrinking.

It is as if looking at both sides of buying a house. The real estate agent and the buyer have very different perspectives of the transaction of buying/selling a house. The real estate agent wants the highest price (because the real estate

Child Nutrition Ratios

	FY 2012–13 Expenditures	FY 2013–14 Expenditures	FY 2014–15 Expenditures	FY 2015–16* Expenditures	
Revenue	$ 4,192,620.59	$ 4,256,467.60	$ 3,869,516.00	$ 4,198,424.86	
Per Pupil Expense	$ 671.36	$ 687.75	$ 644.92	$ 705.62	
Local	$ 300,514.26	$ 277,402.40	$ 252,184.00	$ 273,619.64	
PPE	$ 4.89	$ 44.82	$ 42.03	$ 45.99	
Federal	$ 3,833,839.72	$ 3,972,890.90	$ 3,611,719.00	$ 3,918,715.12	
PPE	$ 613.91	$ 641.93	$ 601.95	$ 658.61	
Vending	$ 3,649.23	$ 3,704.80	$ 3,368.00	$ 3,654.28	
PPE	$ 0.58	$ 0.60	$ 0.56	$ 0.61	
Other	$ 2,432.46	$ 2,469.50	$ 2,245.00	$ 2,435.83	
PPE	$ 0.39	$ 0.40	$ 0.37	$ 0.41	
Cost					
Food	$ 1,622,502.42	$ 1,545,240.40	$ 1,404,764.00	$ 1,524,168.94	
PPE	$ 259.81	$ 249.68	$ 234.13	$ 256.16	
Labor - Salaried	$ 424,007.23	$ 441,674.20	$ 401,522.00	$ 435,651.37	
PPE	$ 67.90	$ 71.36	$ 66.92	$ 73.22	
Labor - Hourly	$ 1,727,138.66	$ 1,501,859.70	$ 1,365,327.00	$ 1,481,379.80	
PPE	$ 276.56	$ 242.67	$ 227.55	$ 248.97	
Labor - Admin	$ 92,225.43	$ 97,079.40	$ 88,254.00	$ 66,190.50	
PPE	$ 14.77	$ 15.69	$ 14.71	$ 11.12	
Supplies	$ 130,205.28	$ 132,188.10	$ 120,171.00	$ 130,385.54	
PPE	$ 20.85	$ 21.36	$ 20.03	$ 21.91	
Repair & Maintenance Cost	$ 46,641.92	$ 47,352.20	$ 33,823.00	$ 36,697.96	
PPE	$ 7.47	$ 7.65	$ 5.64	$ 6.17	
Other Cost	$ 281,086.99	$ 285,367.50	$ 259,425.00	$ 281,476.13	
PPE	$ 45.01	$ 46.11	$ 43.24	$ 47.31	
Total Cost	$ 3,980,005.38	$ 4,040,614.60	$ 3,673,286.00	$ 3,985,515.31	
PPE	$ 637.31	$ 652.87	$ 612.21	$ 669.83	
# of Children	6245	6189	6000	5950	

*Budget Amount

Figure 5.2 Child Nutrition Revenues and Expenses Expressed Per Pupil

agent is compensated on a commission basis), whereas the buyer wants the lowest price. Therefore, it is important to understand what position or lens is being used to view the transaction(s).

Looking at the top line, it is important to look at revenue as a whole and as separate categories. Please remember that the per-pupil amount is the key place to start because that number takes into count a rise or drop in enrollment and keeps numbers relative. When looking at the total revenue number, if it is decreasing per pupil then the sections that create the total revenue can be separated.

Is it the revenue from the federal sources or has vending services taken a large drop? Once the specific source is found, then a plan can be made to either increase the revenue or look at cutting expenditures to match the decline in revenue.

Not to get too complicated but unlike restaurants or other food-serving establishments, cafeterias have a distinct feature that lead them to be more flexible and adaptable to change. These restaurants and other establishments may have high fixed costs; rent and/or mortgage is the highest expense in this category.

The thing with fixed costs is that they have to be paid regardless of revenues or how busy the restaurant/establishment is. CN departments ordinarily do not have these fixed costs.

Therefore, the majority of their costs are variable—which means they can be corrected when there is a drop in revenue. Food cost can have many signs of trouble and this is probably the second biggest source of expenditures behind labor. If the cost is rising, this leads to less profit: Profit = Revenue − Expenditures (costs); therefore, algebraically speaking, the rise in cost with revenue staying constant means less profit.

Food cost can increase by either a rise in the actual cost or if the portion sizes have increased in the cafeterias. To tell the difference is to look at some stable items purchased by the CN department and look at their trend year after year, and if they go up, then you can see if the cost is increasing. If not, then it can be portion size; the line workers are giving too much food or there is too much food being made, leading to waste. One thing that may contribute to this may be theft as well.

Telling the difference between giving too much portions would lead to an unlikely place—the trash can. Is the food being thrown out by the children or by the workers? The simplest way to figure this out, without digging through the trash, is to calculate the number of children that are planning to be served and multiply that by the serving size.

Then take the amount created before service and then the amount left over. Is there some left over? If so, is it more than the projected amount? If yes, then was there too much made in the beginning? If there is less than the amount projected, then the overage was given to the students.

For example, let's say on today's menu is meatloaf, and we are planning to serve 400 students four ounce portions each, so we would need 1,600 ounces of meatloaf. However, 2,000 ounces were made. At the end of the shift there was none left over.

Since there should have been 400 ounces left over, it is safe to say that the extra amount went to the students. Therefore, if the food cost is too high relative to other districts or previous years in the same district, the reason for this increase is the portions are too generous for the students.

Remember that this part of the school district is for-profit, and it should be ran as so or every stakeholder in the district should know that there is a planned loss in CN to compensate for environmental factors such as the need to feed every child more than the charged price of the meal will allow.

Drilling deeper into all of the numbers will provide similar insights. It is important to break labor out if it is deemed an opportunity through benchmarking or previous years' comparison. As the spreadsheet shows labor can be broken out into three different parts: salaried (usually managers, supervisors, and directors), administrative (clerical), and hourly (line and prep employees).

Taking a look at salaried personnel, it is important to remember that these costs are akin to a fixed cost which means the district has to pay for this position. With that said, it is imperative to note that this will have peaks and valleys because each additional student will decrease the per-pupil amount because the salaried staff usually does not change with demand fluctuations and the demand comes from the students.

This is important to consider because those ups and down need to be there, especially if demand is dropping. If it is not there, then the salaried staff is not absorbing the appropriate reduction; this could be political in nature so tread lightly.

Next is the administrative portion of the labor costs, and it is important that this number remains constant because whether the demand is rising or falling administrative support is key to an efficient operation. The reason administrative staff is key is because they tend to be the oil that keeps the engine moving as far as ordering and scheduling.

However, keep in mind that if the district is losing money, then it should make sure that the administrative labor expense compares with districts that are profitable.

Finally, if hourly employees expense, and it will be large, is out of alignment, it could be for one of two reasons: two high of an hourly wage or too many hours worked. The way to figure out if the hourly rate is too high is to look at how many person hours are needed to run the cafeteria; if that amount of hours is what is being worked and the per-pupil amount is too high, then the wage is too high.

The way to calculate the amount of hours needed to run a cafeteria is to look at prep times for recipes and service times for students. Then compare those times to the length of the shift. For simplicity reasons look at a cafeteria that requires 16 hours of prep time and service time is 2 hours with 2 people working the lines and 2 people running food up to the service line. Also, there needs to be a dishwasher for 6 hours.

Therefore, there needs to be 30 hours a day at this particular school (16 for meals, 4 hours for service, 4 hours for running, and 6 hours for washing dishes). If an analysis is done and there are 34 hours being worked in one day at this school, then the variance has been identified.

However, if their costs/expenses are in line with the district that is being benchmarked then that means there may not be enough revenue, money coming in, to cover the costs, but this would come out in the test of the revenue per pupil against other districts or over a period of years at the same district.

Supplies and materials are important also; if this number is too high, then look at the invoices that are coded to this area to see what are the majority of the expenditures tied to, and then look for pockets of waste or things that are not necessary to the core function of serving students delicious meals at a profit!

CONCLUSION

Feeding children nutritious and delicious meals should be at the core of the strategic plan. Children who are not hungry learn better. This chapter looked at how to make that happen. Profitability can happen through appearance, amenities, shrewd business decisions, and knowing what the numbers mean.

Feeding students can be a delicate subject, but if the whole process is done correctly by looking at the CN department through the lens of needing to be profitable and offering compassion through smart decisions, such as a less evasive free and reduced-lunch process at higher grades, the awkwardness of needing to make money off of children can be avoided.

Profitability can erase that awkwardness. Profitability will happen automatically through reduced expenses and increased revenue through increased participation.

Chapter 6

Maintenance and Operation of Plant Ratios

The maintenance department plays a crucial role in the school district. The two most important reasons to look at maintenance are that there may be a huge savings potential and the items that are paid for out of their budget should truly relate to student achievement. This chapter ends with a discussion about the long-term facilities plan and how that can benefit student achievement.

THE NUTS AND BOLTS OF MAINTENANCE

The definition of maintenance for this book will be as follows:

- Custodians—Those wonderful people that work to keep the schools clean
- Utilities—Water, electricity, sewer, trash, natural gas, and so on, and the bills associated with those functions
- Contracted services—Paying an outside company to perform routine tasks, fire extinguisher service, and/or air filter changing
- Payroll costs—Costs associated with the skilled and unskilled labor within the maintenance department
- Administrative payroll costs—Costs associated with the administrative services portion of maintenance
- Supplies and materials—Anything used to help the maintenance department accomplish its goals that is noncapitalized (over a certain cost threshold determined by the district)
- Capital outlay—The fund that is used for major construction renovation or new construction
- Vehicle costs—Costs associated with vehicles used by the maintenance department

How do the above items contribute to student achievement? Quite simply they set the stage for learning.

They are the environmental factors that help students feel comfortable and safe. The comfortable aspect comes from temperature settings and cleanliness, whereas the safety aspect is derived from either things put in place to deter intruders such as fencing or surveillance or plans of actions that are in place to help prevent casualties.

A drop in these costs could lead to a drop in test scores. It is important to remember that no matter the size of the district or the school, every child needs to feel comfortable, safe, and secure.

Maintenance expenses are also a significant part of the budget, and it is important to view maintenance as a key to save money through efficiency. Another, and sometimes unpopular, way to save money in this particular budget is to outsource. The majority of the cost savings comes from not having to pay employer matching costs that are associated with the district having its own employees. These costs include, but are not limited to retirement, health insurance, and social security. These costs can start at 23 percent of the employees' gross wages.

The initial place to start with maintenance data is to see what the trends are. For this process it should be looked at through two different lenses. The first lens is efficiency; if the cost of utilities is rising per student, then that should be investigated more. It is also helpful to look at the utilities per building also separating them by actual activity provided.

In figure 6.1, electricity is continuing to trend upward; therefore, it is necessary to look at the figures on a per-school basis to see which schools are actually causing, or contributing the most to, the increase.

The second perspective is how to use this data to predict student achievement. As mentioned before, students need certain environmental measures to perform academically. The most relevant measures for maintenance are cleanliness, security, climate, and facilities.

	Utilities Per Pupil				
	12–13	13–14	14–15	15–16*	
# of pupils	6100	6150	6200	6175	
Electricty	$ 71.31	$ 88.41	$ 109.63	$ 137.59	
Gas	$ 20.23	$ 17.13	$ 19.20	$ 20.89	
Water	$ 1.90	$ 2.58	$ 2.62	$ 2.84	
Trash	$ 8.22	$ 8.29	$ 8.18	$ 8.62	
Natural Gas	$ 16.16	$ 16.47	$ 16.87	$ 16.58	

Figure 6.1 Yearly Utility Expenses *Budgeted Amount

Cleanliness is imperative because it not only eliminates distractions such as trash, pests, and safety hazards, but can also create a sense of pride for staff and students. With staff, the pride associated with cleanliness can cause an increase in staff attendance because the staff wants to be in a pleasant environment.

It goes without saying how important it is to have staff present and accounted for on a daily basis. The same can be said for students, if they are proud of their school, they want to attend. Therefore, on those days when the student may want to stay in bed, that sense of pride could be the driving force that gets them out of bed and to school.

Security has a wide scope, not only for the inherent characteristics of it but to provide a safe place to facilitate learning. It also lowers risk and future financial obligations that may take purchasing power away from other curriculum-focused projects. Furthermore, safety may not create a safe sense of pride because to talk about safety is to think about the bad things that can happen when safety parameters are breached.

Safety does provide a sense of well-being, and quite frankly, with some at-risk populations, the school may be the safest place the child will be all day. Therefore, safety maybe difficult to measure, but it is a necessity to an environment where teachers can foster a caring environment and students can relax and enjoy themselves while learning.

Security takes on many roles: keeping the staff and students safe from external threats and from each other. Safety is difficult to talk about, but there needs to be a sense of security, whether it is a sophisticated camera system or staff members on duty at specific places throughout the school to prevent acts such as bullying and theft.

The key here is creating an environment that is cost-effective and functional. This environment can be created by having a passion for safety or a tone at the top about safety. If the staff and students know it is a priority, then it will be a priority.

Finally, having safety as a priority can eliminate possible legal fees in the future and those payments that could be made to lawyers could take instructional supplies out of students' hands.

Climate has to do with feeling comfortable. However, the key to climate is being consistent. There are behavioral programs that focus on certain temperature points throughout the day, basically keeping the heat down and the air conditioning high.

For example, an English classroom at the high school is always at the same temperature for the appropriate season. That way students and staff can plan and dress accordingly. When people feel hot or cold, they become irritable and do not perform to their optimal level. This can happen if a staff member plans that his or her classroom will be cold, and he or she dresses accordingly;

however, if for some reason it is hot, and the staff member did not dress up in layers, he or she will have to stay uncomfortable for the entire day.

Sometimes, it takes only one interaction to make a relationship go sour or grow, and if a staff member is irritable, the interactions between staff and student may make the students feel bitter due to the staff's irritability because they are uncomfortable.

The staff usually cannot control the climate, and it is dependent upon the maintenance department to have the ability to foresee any drastic temperature changes and plan accordingly knowing that consistency is critical. This process can be automated with controls that are operated from a central location. The initial investment can be significant, but if implemented for energy conservation, the payback period or the period to re-coup the initial investment should be within ten years.

Facilities or the actual building structure and layout are major contributors to student achievement, the main reason being the ease of use and functionality. One major problem is that new construction is usually tailored to the latest research.

The life of a school building could be fifty years, which is potentially way longer than any educational research tactics. Therefore, it is imperative that new constructions have a flexible design, perhaps able to morph into a number of different configurations or the district will be burdened with the debt of a building that does not function properly.

Existing facilities contribute to the learning environment of the students. One of the more pressing issues is capacity and the lack thereof. It is important to do a capacity study frequently, ensuring that all space is maximized across the district. Mobile classrooms are usually the quick fix if capacity is maximized throughout the district. Beware, mobile classrooms may become detached from the rest of the school because of their location outside of the school walls.

Another point is that sometimes mobile classrooms are rented or leased and then it is important to evaluate that cost versus new construction. Really evaluating the very minimum of purchasing the mobile units outright. Also quite simply don't forget the cost of the connectors that needs to connect the main school building to the mobile unit(s) and protect the students from the weather when changing classes.

BENCHMARKING

There is prominent number that is used in maintenance forecasting and that is 110,000 sq. ft. of school building space per maintenance worker. The origin of this number is unknown and may or may not be the most applicable number. A lot of different factors go into the necessary size of the maintenance department.

The main contributing factor could be the age of the buildings that are in the district. Another factor is the experience level of the actual worker, which lends itself to higher productivity rates.

This is where year-after-year analysis helps. The district could measure the expense per pupil to make sure that the cost was steadily increasing per pupil. Furthermore, if an average age of all of the buildings could be established, then the district could look at other districts with the same average age of buildings and look at their cost per pupil.

Two things would be needed for this calculation from the district's five-year facilities plan (in some states this plan is required by law). On this report, the average age of the building should be stated. The second piece of the puzzle is the audited financial statements. The figure for expenditures on maintenance should be listed by purpose. Also, the number of pupils in the district should be listed in either the facilities plan or the financial statements.

Once this information is gained, an analysis can be done about the expenditures per pupil by simply taking into account the maintenance expenditures and dividing it by the number of students.

A spreadsheet can be compiled region wide or statewide, and then an average can be created by its respective location. Finally, once there is an average, there can be a specific district-to-district comparison or a district-to-regional/state average—both are great benchmarks.

COST AVOIDANCE

Before moving forward looking at saving money, it is important to look at and discuss cost avoidance. Cost avoidance is the idea that improvements in equipment can save money on utility bills. However, it is not real money per se, and the definition of real money in this case is the ability to lower the budget and divert money elsewhere.

For example, if there is a director's position and the person is no longer employed with the district and, the key is, the position will not be filled, then the amount of director's salary can be eliminated from the budget.

Furthermore, cost avoidance is the idea that the expense will not go up and the difference between the old expense and inflation minus the new expense is cost avoidance. In other words the utility expense will not increase from its current level.

The reason this is important is because sometimes commercial vendors will boast about the ability to save money with certain upgrades and or enhancements for a certain dollar amount. In other words, buy this piece of equipment for $200K and save 20K a year on utility expense. That 20K may be cost avoidance; therefore, there may be a 20K reduction in the first year whereas in the second year, it may only be 17K because there is a point of inflation that should be considered because inflation raises utility costs.

With all that a firm may say that they can save the district 50K a year on utilities, with a total investment of 500K and that the total project investment can be paid off in ten years at a payment of 50K a year. However, as time goes on, inflation will erode that 50K and new money will need to be continually infused into the utility budget.

PERFORMANCE CONTRACTING

A way to finance long-term capital needs is through performance contracting, especially those dealing with plant operations or the operation of the buildings themselves (e.g., chillers, boilers, and other heating ventilation air conditioning (HVAC) items). In a nutshell, a performance contract is where a school district contracts with a firm to look at saving money on utility bills through installing more efficient equipment.

The performance contracting firm brings in engineers to look at the functionality of the existing plant equipment. They make a list of recommendations and estimate the amount of savings that will be realized if the upgrades are completed.

They also serve as a conduit to obtain the necessary financing to complete the projects, which is usually in millions of dollars. For example, a performance contracting firm may say they can save 150K annually in utility spending by making 1.5 million dollars in repairs and upgrades (table 6.1). Therefore, taking out interest costs for simplicity, a school district can enter into an agreement with a ten-year note stating that they can pay for said note through energy savings and the performance management company guarantees the savings. Sounds simple enough; however, there are a few caveats.

In the beginning the engineers ask for schedules of when the buildings will be open for use. If the schedule provided to them is not accurate, maybe the school is open for more community night functions, than the person preparing the report knows about; then there is a problem in the calculations because the engineers base their plans on the information provided and that said information is not accurate.

The engineers are forecasting the savings based on operational hours, and when the building is not in use the energy consumed is planned as being greatly decreased. If there are occupants in the building when it is scheduled

Table 6.1 Performance Contracting Simple Analysis

	Year 0	Year 1	Year 2	Year 3	Year 4
Energy spread ($)	3,000,000	1,500,000	1,560,000	1,622,400	1,687,296
Note payable ($)	N/A	1,500,000	1,500,000	1,500,000	1,500,000
Total ($)	3,000,000	3,000,000	3,060,000	3,122,400	3,187,296

to be closed, the schedules of energy uses will not be accurate because more resources will be used by the residents, whether it is the HVAC or running water. Once the initial agreement is signed, very rarely is it changed because the performance contracting company has the burden of guaranteed savings.

There is also specific temperature points that need to be adhered to, and if they are not followed that will affect the amount of savings. Furthermore, the difference caused by the higher or lower temperatures generates more activity from the heating and cooling units which cuts into the savings—once the temperature points are violated, that violation or difference in cost becomes a liability of the school district.

Some of the savings is cost avoidance. There is still going to be an increase in the utility spend budget due to inflation (see figure 6.1). It can be misunderstood that once a performance contract is enacted that utility spend will drop and that is just not the case in an inflationary environment (4 percent a year). Actual use may drop or flat line, but the cost of the applicable service, whether it is water or electricity has the tendency to rise due to inflation.

If the district decides to enter into a performance contract, it is important to look at the time that is projected for the buildings to be open (it is better to error on the high side) and look at the temperature points the agreement is requiring the thermostats to be set at. Those two things can make or break a performance contract if the contract is set up on unrealistic expectations.

CONSTRUCTION MANAGEMENT

Construction management is almost the same except the district goes and gets its own financing as opposed to the performance contracting company in a performance contract, which facilitates that process.

Another difference is there is no guarantee in construction management, whereas with a performance contract, there is a guarantee of savings. A pro of construction management is that with the guarantee from performance contracting, there is also a fee and with construction management, there is not such a steep fee associated with the projects.

FACILITIES PLAN (5 YEARS)

For strategic planning purposes, there needs to be a long-term plan constructed to ensure proper budgeting procedures. In other words, the facilities plan should be a prioritized plan with projects ranked and cost estimates attached. A district should be able to communicate their requirement of priority projects (very important projects) at a cost of X amount of dollars as opposed to communicating that there is a great need for facilities in this district.

When a new budget is created for capital needs, the projects chosen should come from the prioritized list. Furthermore, the plan should be created with community stakeholders to have the proper buy-in, from the community, before a request for funding is even made.

All aspects of operational services should be included: transportation, maintenance, capital outlay, technology, and child nutrition, to name a few. Finally the facilities plan needs to be aligned with the strategic plan. For example, if the strategic plan calls for technology in every student's hand, then the facilities plan should have the schedules and costs to do that.

CONCLUSION

Maintenance is key to a school district's success, because it is the facilitator of temperature, appearance, facility upkeep, cleanliness, and safety. Maintenance is also a huge part of the budget and needs to be monitored for efficiency. There are external factors that can be considered to help the maintenance budget such as performance contracts and construction management. The facilities plan is the lynch pin for long-term capital planning.

Chapter 7

Transportation Ratios

The transportation department can be the first thing the children of a district see and the last thing they see before they go home. Therefore, with that type of visibility, between the transportation department and the children, it goes without saying how important it is. It contributes directly to both student achievement and the bottom line of the school district. It is based on safety and reliability.

This chapter looks to define the direct relationship between transportation and student achievement. The financial side of the department will also be looked at with the primary function of examining cash flow because lowering cash flow will lead to a reduction in expenditures.

Transportation is one of those auxiliary services that has to be conducted; it is an inherent obligation for public schools. The sweet spot is to operate a transportation department within the allocated budget and provide excellent customer service.

HOW DOES TRANSPORTATION DIRECTLY AFFECT STUDENT ACHIEVEMENT?

The short answer is through reliability. The reason reliability is critical is because parents and students need to know that their bus will arrive within a certain timeframe. If the parents cannot trust the reliability of the buses, they may choose to take the child to school, which becomes a time liability.

With the expectation the child was going to be on the bus, the district is in control of what time the child will arrive at school. When the parent takes control of that situation, the district is at the mercy of that parent to get their child to school on time.

This becomes an issue, because even though the majority of parents respect the need of their child's education, they do not understand the critical nature that instructional time plays related to a child's academic growth.

Just think if a child misses just 15 minutes of instructional time on half the days in a 180-day school calendar, 90 days, then 225 hours of instructional time is lost, but hey, it's just 15 minutes, right?

There are probably a select few parents who are habitually late. Therefore, it is important for the school and the transportation department to communicate so that the district can rebuild that trust with those parents. The reason this is important is because if those families can be targeted, the amount of truancy could be dramatically decreased school or district wide.

As a side note, with these particular parents, the ones with truancy issues, special attention can be paid. For example, send them some sort of communication early in the morning, such as a wakeup call. This way they can wake up early and have plenty of time to help their child get ready for school.

SAFETY

Safety is one of those non-negotiable criteria that a school district has; parents trust the district with the safety of their children, and it is important the district lives up to that expectation. Safety on the bus is twofold. First is traffic safety, not driving recklessly and losing control of the school bus, along with safety from other drivers. Second is safety from the children themselves, such as fighting, bullying, or other issues between the students.

It goes without saying that the school bus drivers can be one of the lowest paying jobs in a school district and have an awful large amount of responsibility. Therefore, it is critical that time and resources are invested in training and background checks of the drivers.

There needs to be a balance between safety and convenience for the parent. Convenience is a necessary evil because once riding the bus becomes an inconvenience, then the parent will do anything to eliminate it.

There have been many technical updates that can alert parents when their child's bus will arrive via their cell phone. Those technical updates are a powerful tool because they add convenience and do not jeopardize safety.

To take the technical updates to another level, these updates are not free so where does a district find the funds to pay for such conveniences that will more than likely help parents out and may actually increase participation for children riding buses, which may decrease tardiness and increase student achievement?

Staff and labor costs are the only place this can come from. The technical update could reduce phone calls, and this would lead to an opportunity to reduce office staff through attrition to realize the savings to pay for the updates.

What is the district/department/school willing to give up to get something new? This is a classic question. Too many times in education there is no new funding for new initiatives, even though there is real value in the technical updates/initiatives. Hence districts need to get creative so that they can stay relevant with stagnant funding.

It is also important to look at the negative side of things and what bus drivers can do to cheat the system or in other words, cost the district money.

Time creep is one of the biggest issues in two ways; sometimes the drivers will leave the bus running in idle while they too sit idle in an undisclosed location away from school property or in the school parking lot. Therefore, the drivers are running up expenses in two categories: payroll—because they are on the clock—and fuel—because the bus is still running.

A standard should be set indicating that the behavior associated with time creep and the lack of understanding with regard to safety will not be tolerated, and infractions will be dealt with severely and swiftly.

STRATEGIES TO SAVE MONEY IN TRANSPORTATION

There are numerous ways to save money in transportation, but a lot of them can come with public/parent backlash. Therefore, first the tweaks that should not cause major backlash will be covered and then the potentially upsetting tactics will be covered.

Global Positioning System (GPS)

Putting GPS on buses covers the low-hanging fruit. These devices may cost a lot up front or a significant monthly payment for leased options. They are worth it though. They now give the district the leverage to see where every bus is in the district and what functions the buses are performing in real time.

For example, some programs have the power to show remotely when a stop-arm has been activated. The GPS units usually pay for themselves in efficiency savings and the safety extras are gravy.

The efficiency savings come from lower fuel and lower payroll costs because the GPS monitors the period of idleness of the bus. Some GPS software packages alert the main user if there is any variance from the standard route in time or miles.

Once the route is tightened up, the payroll savings is incurred also because the drivers cannot elude the system and pull off and stay idle somewhere.

Let us move on to the changes that could lend themselves to a bit of growing pains. Please remember that the easiest way to find money is to create savings. Therefore, the gain with these changes will be worth the pain when the dollars saved can be diverted back into curriculum and instruction.

Corner Stops

This idea is fairly simple to put in place and has the biggest bang for its buck in rural areas. This involves stopping the bus at a predetermined location, such as a bus stop, as opposed to stopping in front of a child's house. The growing pains come from parents being used to picking up their child in front of their house, and with corner stops, they have to walk to that location.

Furthermore, some safety issues may arise because it is farther to walk to a bus stop than it is to walk to the bus that is stopped right outside the house.

Corner stops save time, which translates into savings for fuel, wear and tear on buses, and payroll expenditures, because the driver can do the route faster with less stops.

Staggered Routes

This cost-cutting strategy is effective when looking to save costs on the actual number of buses in a fleet and also realize some other efficiencies along the way. The growing pains are that some students have to wake up much earlier than other children at different stages of school (elementary, middle school, and high school). It is critical to align the bell schedules of the schools to the staggered schedule as well.

How staggered routes work is that the same bus runs routes for two or three different schools in the same period of the day. For example, in the morning the same bus and driver may drive for an elementary school, a middle school, and maybe even a high school.

The savings on the actual buses come from the need to only have one bus for several different schools as opposed to having a bus per school per route. There is also some cost savings on labor for drivers as there is little transition time because typically the same driver stays with the bus for all of the routes.

Inventory and Cash Flow

Inventory is an important metric to watch. The reason it is important is because it is imperative that certain parts are on hand to keep the bus garage smoothly rolling; however, when the actual cash is spent on a part, it means that the cash is gone and if the part does not get used promptly, then that cash has lost its purchasing power.

Therefore, making an expenditure on a piece of inventory that is not critical to the mission of the transportation department can be equated to throwing actual cash in a trash can. This comes about because the expenditures take up a limited resource, cash, and turns it into something that may not be usable. That cash could have been used on something more curriculum and strategic plan focused.

Theft

A less than positive side to some employees is that they cannot control the darker side of their personalities. Theft at a bus garage is easy and can go undetected if efficient systems are not in place. The ease of theft comes from the fact that the bus garages uses similar things that a person's own automobile uses. Some examples of theft are oil, tires, and garage time.

A standard practice is to put cases of oil on service trucks and then not account for them as the oil is used off of the trucks in the field. A lot of times oil may be used, but not on a vehicle that is property of the school district.

A way to prevent this is to have a check-in and check-out system for cases of oil and monitor usage. A standard baseline should be implemented for the use of oil and any variances should be investigated.

Even though bus tires cannot be used on personal vehicles, they can be a staple on the theft list. A common thing that happens is that a new tire will be taken off of the rack and be replaced by an old tire so that, at a glance, the rack will look full. There are two ways to stop this. First, inspect the new tires on the rack and keep a good inventory. Second, monitor the tires that are to be disposed of, ensuring their prompt disposal.

MEASURING COST IN THE TRANSPORTATION DEPARTMENT

What are some of the ways that the transportation department can be financially measured? There are two predominant methods to look at the financial aspects of the transportation department. First is checking if the department is staying within budget. Many states directly provide the transportation funding. Those states have metrics to determine the amount of funding the districts receive.

If the transportation expense is greater than the allotted funds from the state, if applicable, then there is a problem that needs to be investigated further. Furthermore, if there is a local formula on how to allocate funding to the transportation department, then the formula is tested for soundness. That local formula should be regarded in the same manner as those school districts that receive the funding from the state.

If there is an excess of funds needed from other sources to balance the transportation department's budget, then the ratios need to be created. First create the ratios for the overall department: total expenditures divided by the number of children. Then benchmark other districts. Please remember that the funding for the transportation department should be listed by the audit report as well as the number of children in the district. Using the same mathematical formula, one could derive the cost per pupil from other districts with the respective districts audit reports.

If there is a district that operates more efficiently, then it may be time to give them a call to see how the rest of their expenditures break down. The audit report only goes into so much detail. It is important to look at several cost drivers to figure out which metric is not in line with other districts. Those cost drivers are fuel, parts, labor, or other costs (this being anything else not identified in the first three areas).

Another option is to check if the previous years supplied a break-even mark or a surplus of funds; the school district can then benchmark itself and see what cost drivers increased. Once the cost driver is identified, it can be reasoned to identify the actual culprit of the increased cost. That area can be corrected, and this will make the transportation department more fiscally successful.

STAFF

A significant expense to the transportation department is the staff that enables it to run. It goes from the hourly paid bus drivers to the director. Consequently, there is a lot of room for inefficiencies. Something that can be done to maximize efficiency is to ensure that the bus routes are optimally constructed at the beginning of the year. The bus routes should be designed so that the bus is spending the shortest possible amount of time on the road.

The number of actual staff members can be irrelevant in this case, if they are hourly paid—majority of the time bus drivers are hourly workers as opposed to salary workers. The key if they are hourly is the pay rate. Sometimes the pay rate is set, like in the situation of a unionized bus garage.

If the transportation department is not unionized, then the department can immediately begin to cut costs through new hires by paying less. If the department is part of a union, then during the next negotiation period, sustainability can be discussed.

The tactic of paying someone less may seem harsh, but it is better than not spending on a child's education. The interesting thing about public education is the number of parameters that go into the actual process of educating the child. Therefore, it is critical to be sure that every resource is maximized.

CONCLUSION

It is obvious that the transportation department is critical to any district's strategic mission and goals. However, it is not so obvious the factors that go into the financial well-being of the department.

If there are financial issues, then look at staff, fuel, or supplies. Benchmark those results either against previous years or districts that have the same demographics.

Safety and convenience should not be overlooked. They are the catalysts for student achievement. They are absolutely critical to the district's overall performance.

Finally, there are some things that can be put in place, but they cost money. However, they can open the door for a parent to feel comfortable about letting their child ride the buses, which leads to less truancy from the parents and more instructional time available for the student.

Chapter 8

Technology Ratios

Technology can be the missing link for engagement. The bottom line is that technology is a tool that majority of schools districts use to engage their students. With that high level of expectation comes a lot of responsibility. This chapter digs deep into the financial aspect of technology and how to mitigate through the risks that could be associated with a major technology purchase and deployment.

WHERE TO START?

Technology and student achievement go hand in hand two ways: by making the learning engaging and by giving a method to track progress. Technology requires a substantial investment.

The lynchpin to any great financial investment is the plan behind it. The plan can take two forms: the budget and a written plan. In the case of technology, there needs to be a district technology plan that starts with strategic and measurable educational goals, preferably from the strategic plan.

Second, there needs to be a budget that reflects the financial obligations of the technology plan and how to execute it. The budget needs to be reasonable with a refresh plan incorporated into the projected expenditures.

The importance of the technology plan cannot be overstated. Within that plan needs to be specific equipment details. As mentioned earlier, the importance lies in efficiency. If there are many different types of computers throughout the district, economies of scale cannot take place.

Economies of scale happens when a process is replicated many times and a cost advantage is achieved. Therefore, if there are a limited number of computer types/brands that the district can purchase, then the district's technicians can achieve much efficiency since they will be working on the same machines over and over.

The technology plan needs to mirror the strategic plan, which aligns to the ultimate goals of the district. The technology plan can elaborate on how to use technology to reach the goals of the district. Especially since technology is a major vehicle to help students learn.

The advantages of technology are numerous; the ability to track data to realize growth is an important piece to the technological puzzle. It streamlines the data collection process and can help tell the story about the children who are using the technology through trend lines and data points. Those trend lines and data points will contribute to decisions that can help the district grow.

A lot of software comes with data-capturing capabilities and a reporting function already built in. Therefore, content and relevance is key to making a successful software program. There are many programs that can be tailored to a whole host of needs, from reading to credit recovery.

When talking about technology, a rise in costs is the first thing that comes to mind, which is true, but there are ways technology can lower the cost of lesson delivery. There are a lot of free applications available at this point in time that many teachers find very useful and engaging.

To improve student achievement is to find the analytics that tell the story of the child and show specifically where that child needs help. A lot of times a child is one or two test questions away from being successful. If there is no tracking mechanism in place, then the child will not have a starting point to grow academically.

OTHER BONUSES OF TECHNOLOGY

Electronic books are a great addition to a district's learning portfolio. The cost savings comes from a zero replacement cost. The academic piece comes from the ease and convenience of electronic books, which can offer many other online resources to go along with additions that may maximize the learning experience.

To keep with the theme in the previous sections, electronic textbooks offer an array of tracking options also, most notably the ability to report how many times the title has been read or checked out of the library, which can help lead the way to maximize future electronic book/textbook purchases.

OPPORTUNITIES WITH TECHNOLOGY

Testing is a multifaceted discussion when dealing with technology. There are some sides that say students are more comfortable with taking a paper and pencil exam, which is quite possible, especially if the network at school is not reliable.

It is common knowledge that testing causes anxiety; therefore, if there is anxiety associated with the network or reliability of the machines, then there could be added anxiety, which is not a recipe for success.

Talk to the stakeholders, especially the students, to find out what the opportunities are within testing, especially in a turnaround school, where every point and correct question helps. It is imperative that before the testing is conducted the situation is assessed to make sure there are enough machines and the network can handle so many machines online at one time.

Just like making sure the sprinklers are turned off for graduation at a high school football stadium, it is important to test the particular area where the testing will happen.

Special attention needs to be paid to the lack of internet connectivity in some poor and rural areas. Some work can be done offline but the at-home connectivity is critical, without which a computer is merely a paperweight, especially machines that are made to go along with an internet service provider and a cloud-type storage mechanism.

Building partnerships with local internet vendors and getting those vendors to buy in can help that cause. It may even be beneficial to monitor the birth rates in certain areas of the district to predict a population boom that perhaps the internet service providers may have missed.

WHAT TYPE OF POSITIONS CAN HELP?

Not only is it important to have a technology department that understands the interworkings of servers, networks, and switches, but it is also important to have a translator that can turn that hardware into student achievement.

Most times that translator is referred to as a person expert in instructional technology. In medium to large districts this position is necessary to facilitate the growth and innovation that a district-wide initiative would entail. In a small district there may need to be positions that cover instructional technology and other areas within curriculum and instruction.

There should also be school-level technology experts to help with instruction and hardware/software issues. Remember that giving a presentation with a computer is not maximizing the potential of that computer or using twenty-first-century practices. It is merely using the computer to replace an overhead projector. That is the reason it is imperative to have an instructional technology expert providing professional development to the teachers and staff.

WHERE DOES THE MONEY COME FROM?

This is where the efficiency indicators for the district come in. Are there programs throughout the district that would use less money if they were run more efficiently? The key is to set benchmarks to other successful districts with the same demographics in areas such as child nutrition, maintenance, and transportation.

The reason for benchmarking is to have a simple method to understand where the improvements can take place. Key elements to benchmarking are the number of students and the audited financial statements. With the number of students and the audited financials, the amount per pupil can be achieved, indicating which district is spending less per pupil.

Once the thriftiness is established, then the indicators will perform their intended process, showing the district where money can be saved. With the savings, the technology plan can be maximized and fulfilled in an accelerated manner.

LEASE OR BUY?

To continue with the business side of things, when looking to purchase a large number of computers, there are several choices to be made, but the main two choices are lease and buy.

The important things to know about a lease is what is its overall cost, the interest rate associated with it, the service plan for the length of the lease, the cost of the machine(s) when the lease is up, and how long is the lease or what are the terms.

Leasing may be the only way to go if the district is strapped for cash and does not have a way to raise a large amount of capital in a short period.

When looking to buy a large number of machines outright, it is important to remember to budget for the refresh process in the years after the initial purchase. Another way to go about it would be to buy a third of the machines at a time if there was a three-year refresh rate or a fourth of the machines in case of a four-year refresh rate. This way the money can be budgeted every year and the machines will get refreshed.

The decision boils down to a couple of options: to purchase the machines outright at one time or lease them over several years (there are other types of lease available to own vehicles). To purchase the machines outright, there needs to be a significant amount of cash in hand, significant infrastructure, and training in place.

Furthermore, with that one-time purchase, money needs to be set aside year after year for a technology refresh plan. Whereas with a lease-type purchase, there is time to set up the network and the training.

SELF-INSURE OR BUY INSURANCE

Insurance is very important for these machines; there are primarily two options: to buy the insurance or to self-insure. Either way there is usually a technology fee charged to the students. That fee either buys the insurance or is used to start the account for self-insurance.

With self-insurance, the money collected acts as the fund to cover any losses. The key is to collect more money than is needed. With larger districts, this works better because there is more money in the pot, thereby reducing the risk that the money collected will not be enough.

In table 8.1, the district with the most children has the most actual dollars left over; therefore, this helps reduce the risk of shortage of funds to repair the machines.

To buy insurance means, the risk of not having enough funds available to pay for any loss is transferred to the insurance company. However, there is a cost associated with that transfer of risk. This leads to the whole point if the district can withstand the risk, then the cost will be lower, and the money it makes for taking that risk can be diverted to purchasing more computers or software.

DIFFERENT GRADES DIFFERENT MACHINES

Within the technology plan needs to be specific instructions on which grades can use which machines. Different grades require different machines. Kindergarteners cannot navigate the keyboard; therefore, they would be more in line with a tablet/touchscreen-type device.

Furthermore, there are different machines for different types of programs, especially at the high school level. There may be in-depth classes being offered that require a more sophisticated machine to conduct the needs of the

Table 8.1 Analysis of Self Insuring Versus Purchasing Insurance

Number of students	3,000	6,000	12,000	18,000
Cost of computers ($300 EA)	$900,000	$1,800,000	$3,600,000	$5,400,000
Insurance costs 5%	$45,000	$90,000	$180,000	$270,000
Fee charged ($25 per student)	$75,000	$150,000	$300,000	$450,000
Difference	$30,000	$60,000	$120,000	$180,000

educational programs, whereas other classes just need the basic machines to keep students engaged.

Technology can help with other opportunities throughout the district such as credit recovery and distant education. Along the lines with credit recovery, it is important to use the technology plan to identify the proper software to align the goals of the district with the functions of the software.

Software can be a major expenditure. Before digging deeper into this idea, it is important to think about buying in bulk. It is important to look at getting a site license for the entire district if the majority of schools use a particular software. Purchasing a license may not be a great strategy every time, but it is important to look into because the per-pupil price can be significantly less.

Furthermore, it is important to realize two things: The first thing is that "stuff" very rarely moves a district forward. Second, when making a large purchase, the district needs a partner as opposed to a vendor and that expectation needs to be expressed up front. While making that point, it may be worthwhile to point out that a vendor can be found anywhere, but partners truly add value.

A partner is an entity that sees a project from its inception to its completion, whereas a vendor is simply an entity that sells goods or services to another entity. With large-scale implementation projects, such as a technology plan, it is important to have a partnership commitment from the purchasing organization. This agreement helps with fidelity.

TECHNOLOGY AND THE BUSINESS SIDE OF THE DISTRICT

Technology can be leveraged in several different ways. Not only is it important to leverage technology for student achievement, but it is also important to leverage it to save money, and the savings can be used to contribute to other programs.

An excellent example is payroll for hourly employees. Having an automated system for payroll can save a significant amount of money. The key is to save the money (actual cash), then lower the budget for the particular function that is saving the money and either budget that money in another area or earmark that savings for year-end savings; see table 8.2.

Table 8.2 Potential Staff Savings

	Beg. budget	Budget adjustments	Ending budget
Hourly employees	$1,500,000	$(250,000)	$1,250,000
Computer software	0	$150,000	$150,000
Instructional tech.	$350,000	$100,000	$450,000
Total budget	$1,850,000	0	$1,850,000

INFRASTRUCTURE

Within the technology plan should be information about specifications of the infrastructure needed to accomplish the goals. It would be a classic example of putting the cart before the horse if a district were to invest heavily in the actual computer machines and not have the network to support the devices.

The number of devices that the network can support is also very important. The key thing to consider here is if there will be a BYOD (bring your own device) piece for daily delivery of instruction. If so, then those devices need to be included in the count of machines to be supported by the network.

Without getting very technical, the network consist of several things: the actual amount of internet that is available to the district and the wireless access points that support the amount of internet coming in.

If the amount of internet coming in is adequate, but the access points cannot handle the number of machines, then there is a constraint. The constraint is the access points and even if, for example, the amount of internet coming supports 3,000 machines but the sum of all the access points is 1,500, then the network will only be able to support the 1,500 machines.

Vice versa can also happen, where the access points are adequate but the amount of internet coming in is not adequate. The constraint, because of the number of machines, is that the internet can support only a limited number of machines as opposed to the access points.

It is imperative to focus on the academic gains that can be achieved through a strong network. The strength of the network corresponds to the trust that the staff will put into the technology itself. It is very easy to go back to old habits when twenty-plus second graders are staring straight ahead because the software that the teacher had planned to teach that day isn't loading.

As mentioned earlier, if funds spent on paper or consumption of paper continues in an area where there has been significant upgrades in technology, the ultimate problem may be lack of teachers who agree with the reliability of the network. Therefore, the strength of the network is the strength of the methods to increase student achievement.

TECHNOLOGY SAFETY

Safety for the students is one of the top priorities of many school districts. Also students need safety measures to protect them from their own curiosity. Keeping the security of the network or the availability for which websites is a good stopgap for both predators' and students' curiosity.

There needs to be a way for teachers to access some websites that may not be ideal for students to visit. Therefore, a login system is needed to differentiate end users from staff and students.

The ability to track users and locations within the district is important. The importance lies in the positive and negative. The positive aspect is the ability to track data and progress by user. The negative piece is in case somebody sends a negative message or threat.

HOW TO TELL IF IT IS WORKING?

This is a very simple process; as mentioned earlier, an increase in the amount spent on technology should show a decrease in supply (especially paper) spending. If there is absence of inverse relationship and the budget codes or the account where the money is spent from is named different names, then there is a lack of buy-in.

Figure 8.1 shows how the relationship should work between supplies and technology purchases. The per-pupil number is the most important for the respective categories because it keeps all the data relative. If the opposite is happening, then the probable cause, even if the amount spent on supplies, is the same as a lack of buy-in for the new or expanding technology.

INVENTORY

It is important to have a proper tracking and inventory system in place. In theory someone in the district should be able to pull a report and have a reasonable chance at knowing how many machines are there and in what locations.

Not only is this important from the standpoint of asset protection to not over order. A good inventory system helps to prevent over ordering. The system does this by giving a frame of reference to cross check any new orders. For example, a school may order devices for a third grade classroom(s). The purchasing or technology department could pull the inventory and validate the accuracy of the order and prevent over ordering. Over ordering is not fiscally responsible and can weaken an asset protection plan.

Furthermore, there should be a detailed plan instructing the schools how much it will cost to refresh their machines on the scale that is set forth by the technology plan. This will give visibility to the expenditure and simplify the budgeting process.

Finally, there should be a go-to guide for the district for different software applications from the curriculum department. Once the specific needs of the child are established, there should be an easy-to-use guide that points

	Elementary School A			
	2014–15	2015–16	2016–17*	
Number of students	475	495	485	
Supplies and materials	$ 15,000.00	$ 11,000.00	$ 7,500.00	
Per Pupil	$ 31.58	$ 22.22	$ 15.46	
Computer hardware	$ 30,000.00	$ 40,000.00	$ 48,000.00	
Per pupil	$ 63.16	$ 80.81	$ 98.97	
Computer software	$ 5,500.00	$ 7,500.00	$ 8,000.00	
Per pupil	$ 11.58	$ 15.15	$ 16.49	
* Budget				

Figure 8.1 Expenditures Per Pupil

principals and teachers in the correct direction for what software can help with a specific need. For example, if the child has an issue with comprehension and its word count is low, the principal could find which software program is vetted by the district to help address those opportunities.

CONCLUSION

To have children ready for the next chapter in their lives, it is critical that everyone is on board with technology, because technology is going to be intertwined in their lives.

The first place to start to ensure technology's presence is the strategic plan; then, off of that plan, the technology plan should detail all facets of the technology for the school district.

Do not forget the business side of technology because it can help to save or redirect funds to other critical instructional areas.

Finally, it is important to remember the inventory procedures and that if there is flat or increased per-pupil spending on supplies and materials (paper) paired with an increase in technology, it would mean that there is potentially a lack of buy-in from the staff. Owing to the nature of an increase in technology inherently means a decrease in the use of supplies and materials (paper).

Chapter 9

Other Ratios to Consider

The critical step to educating a child is focusing on the internal and external factors, such as mental and physical health. Those external factors are important importance to educating the entire student is critical. However, the costs need to be monitored, to be fiscally responsible. The same cost information can be used to predict student achievement through benchmarking and year-after-year comparisons.

Each department that will be discussed, such as exceptional children (EC), testing, and student services, has its share of expenditures. The key is the return received from those expenditures and how can that data be used to predict student achievement.

Furthermore, the mission statements of those departments should match with that of the district's strategic plan. Their budget should mirror those mission statements and the expenditures should align with the budget.

If those steps are locked in, then student achievement can be reached. Even though money isn't the answer to student achievement, spending money to educate and foster the whole child is.

EXCEPTIONAL CHILDREN

A district cannot move forward unless all of the children move forward. EC is a department that has a significant amount of risk associated with it. Depending on the percentage of children that are considered EC relative to the funding received, there can be a gap.

The gap arises from the necessity to provide services (or face a lawsuit) and the lack of revenue received to support the needed services. There are times when a private or parochial school can better serve the needs of a child than the public school. Even though cost should not be the deciding or leading factor, it could be less expensive to pay for the child to receive services at another school than provide them in-house.

As time goes on and other diagnoses are introduced, it becomes more and more expensive to provide the proper services. Furthermore, it is a necessity, by law, for the children to receive the services they are required to have.

Once a child is found to be EC, then the individual education plan (IEP) needs to be established and within that plan is a list of things that need to be provided to help the child succeed. Sometimes EC is viewed as having an unlimited amount of funds because the services need to be provided. This is true in a sense with a risk-averse district, but in many cases it is just not about the dollars and cents because all districts have finite budgets.

A step to make sense of the expenditure data is to find the cost per pupil for general education and EC combined and then the cost per student for all the children who are considered EC for the previous three years per EC expenditures. Then do the same with the general education expenditures.

Doing a percent change with the general education figures and the EC expenditure features will tell if the cost for EC students is rising at the same rate as the general education expenditures.

Next, have a list sorted by diagnosis of the children with the children's initials (names may violate the Health Insurance and Accoutability Act laws) and diagnosis listed. Total each diagnosis, and compile and compare these numbers for the previous three years.

Next, gather the expenditure data for the previous three years sorted by diagnosis. Make an expense per child per diagnosis. If the expenditure per child per diagnosis is rising year after year, then double check to make sure the number of the children being diagnosed isn't rising as well. If the diagnosis is rising—which is the most expensive one—then the district can expect accelerated costs.

For example, if the number of children diagnosed on the autism spectrum disorder increased, then the next question is: Is that diagnosis expensive? The individual expense can be figured out by taking the number of children diagnosed and dividing it by the actual amount of money spent in a given time period on that diagnosis. This needs to be done with the other diagnosis so that an average by diagnosis can be created.

If autism spectrum disorder is higher per pupil than the average, then it makes sense that the cost per pupil has increased. It is important to strip out the reason the costs has risen because district budgets are a zero-sum game. If one part needs more, it takes from another area.

How can monitoring the cost data affect student achievement directly? The cost data will tell the story of what is being spent and who it is being spent on. For example, if there is an increased diagnosis of autism spectrum disorder, is there an increase in expenditures for materials, professional development, and staff (whose job duty is to work with students with autism) relative to the autism spectrum disorder?

If there are increased costs in materials, professional development, and staff for students who are blind and that segment of the population is decreasing, then there is a disconnect in the way the money is being spent and the students who need the services may not be receiving the services they need.

The contributing factor to student achievement with EC is making sure the funds are going to the students who need it. There is also a significant risk associated with not providing the necessary services if a child's IEP calls for it. The risk is simply a lawsuit from the parent to the school district.

Therefore, the key to predicting student achievement through EC expenditures is associating the diagnosis from the IEP to the funds spent relative to that diagnosis. If there is a correlation, one could predict an increase in expenditures and an insulation from risk because the funds are being properly allocated to the specific need that arises from the appropriate diagnosis and IEP.

The critical balance comes from the need for the district to provide the appropriate services while using the most cost-effective manner. Outsourcing could be the only option in some scenarios but remember that in some cases outsourcing is more expensive than hiring a person. There are certain scenarios where outsourcing is a necessity because there is no one for hire and the services need to be given.

One way to counteract this is to always be recruiting for hard-to-staff areas. Most of the time these outsourced people are independent contractors and if they become employees, there could be some stability for them that they did not have as an independent contractor, such as benefits and a defined work schedule.

TESTING

The testing department is the expert of the data for the district. In a publicly traded company the metric that is looked by investors is the earnings per share (EPS). Test scores are a district's EPS. Investors look for growth in EPS, whereas stakeholders of the school district look for test scores to see how the district is doing and if it is a good investment of tax payers' dollars.

The testing department is a critical piece to the puzzle for new principals and administrators. Therefore, if there is a district where there is a high turnover of veteran principals to new principals, the ability to disseminate testing data is critical. Also, if the district is in high growth, as far as adding buildings, and is adding new principals this is the same circumstance as the district with high turnover. Numerous new principals increase the necessity of the testing department's ability to communicate results, whether from growth or turnover.

Furthermore, creating a culture of promoting within (assistant principal to principal) can help smooth any transitions or turnover. The reason for the smoothing is the assistant or vice principals will already have the tools to disseminate the testing data relative to the specific school district.

Imagine if there was a ticker showing all of the school districts data that is updated in real time to the other schools in the district. Some schools may be hesitant about showing their testing data, but a school district is a school system and not a system of schools. Therefore, showing the data will give the administrators the opportunities to see which schools are being successful and those that have opportunities to grow. Remember collaboration is key to move a district forward.

The testing department is responsible for the communication and the interpretation of the testing data. That data is critical to communicating the districts' successes and opportunities. With the necessity of interpretation, it is important to be able to communicate what the test results actually mean.

To show gains in a short amount of time, it is important to focus on what is commonly referred to as the "bubble kids," those children that are very close to achieving the next tier on a test, whether it is a letter grade (A or B) or a number (3 or 4). The testing department can help find which children can be focused on. Furthermore, the testing department could have strategies to help administrators create plans to help the children who have the most bang for the buck, in other words focusing on moving those bubble children to the next tier.

In business there is a trend to focus on a core group of products. Take Apple Inc., for example; in the late 1980s they had numerous models of Mac PCs, whereas now they have a set of core products. Even though they are expanding on electronic gadgets like the iPad and iPhone into different sizes, they really only have a core amount of products. There is a direct correlation to the success the stockholders have realized (an increase) and the number of products that are offered by Apple (a decrease).

This inverse correlation is from the ability of really intelligent people honing their attention to a small set of deliverables. The interesting piece here is that students are all different; therefore, a lot of really intelligent people are focusing on many different things. However, if the bubble children are focused on, then that will bring an immediate jump in test scores. Because the intelligent people are focusing on the core group of students to achieve an increase in test scores in a short period.

In a time of transition and lack of credibility, a district may choose to stabilize itself by focusing on these bubble kids to add stability while they continually focus on a plan to turn the whole district around.

A way to use the expenditure data from testing to see if there will be an increase or decrease in student achievement looks at staff development program and collaboration. In many areas across the United States testing changes frequently. If there is a decrease in expenditures for the testing department for professional development, then the members of the department may be falling behind the learning curve.

Finally, it costs money in supplies to deliver strong presentations and staff development programs. Therefore, to make sure the testing department is focusing on its core job, facilitating actual testing and communicating those results, there needs to be a continuous stream of expenditures.

With that said, a district leader could see if there is a below average amount of expenditures happening compared to the same period last year. If so, there may be a lack of communication or facilitation of testing data, which is horrible because administrators cannot use their tools to fix problems if they do not know they have them.

STUDENT SERVICES

From the point of this book, student services will consist of mental health workers, guidance counselors, nurses, and social workers. When looking at these pieces, it is important to understand what a decrease in investment means and what should be expected for a constant or increase in investment. The reason they contribute to student achievement will also be mentioned.

These positions act as a filter from the issues of the students' external environment and their academic future. It is important to remember that, even though not by choice, public schools have become the one place students can turn to focus on them as a whole person. Education is changing, especially in urban and high-poverty areas. Children are dealing with more and more issues from abuse to generational poverty.

Mental Health Workers

A decrease or lack of investment in positions with the direct responsibility of providing mental health services can contribute to a higher dropout rate, office referrals, and classroom disruptions. Many times a child who is facing issues from the external environment will mirror the behavior he/she sees—violent or not.

An increase in investment can address dropout rates, office referrals, and classroom disruptions. Furthermore, teacher morale can increase when classroom disruptions are lowered.

One unintended consequence could be that direct classroom instruction could be taken away for the students as they are pulled out for sessions with the mental health workers, but it is better to get the external issues under control so the academic teachings can take root than to leave the student in class, which could lead to more disruptions and affect other students.

An example of sacrificing instructional time for mental health workers is similar to a credit card company running a credit check on a potential card holder. The company wants to make sure everything is in order before it grants the cardholder the ability to use the card, therefore creating a beneficial relationship for the credit card company and the card holder, where the card holder has access to credit, and the credit card, company can possibly generate revenue from interest or other fees.

Moreover, the potential borrower and the credit card company are making sure they have the groundwork laid for a successful business relationship; similarly, a school district must have the groundwork laid for a student to be successful. If the student is not prepared to be successful, then the situation can be akin to building a house in sand.

Guidance Counselors

Guidance counselors play important but different roles at each level of education. In high school they act as gate keepers to the scheduling process and as conduits for a college education and scholarship dollars. In elementary school they teach a full load of classes on character development.

Monitoring the amount spent can act as an insight into the direction of character education, scholarship funds, college, and job placement. It is not only about the position costs but also about the training and staff development program the guidance counselors receive.

If a district needs to see improvement in its students' adjustment into adult life, then there should be an increase in the investment in guidance counselors. By virtue of their position, those increases are at the heart of what they do. It is also very important to hold them accountable for what they do. It is very easy to track their output, especially at the high school level.

When a senior is filling out their graduation questionnaire or exit survey, ask them if a guidance counselor helped them with their college or scholarship application process, or with their job placement.

Furthermore, tracking the actual scholarship dollars per pupil or the number of students going on to college or taking up job placements is a simpler way to track their performance and productivity. The guidance counselors may get some freebies if the students or parents were heavily involved with the process of receiving scholarships, college acceptance, or job placement.

Finally, if there is a drop in expenditure per pupil, then the district can also expect a drop in scholarship dollars, college acceptance, and job placements, three very critical areas that tell the story of educating the whole student and having them ready for the next stage of their life.

Nurses

A nurse's job is critical because her duties needs to happen even if she is not there. If another person is responsible for the nurse's duties that day, then that person may be giving medicines and making diagnoses. More times than not these placeholders, who are usually very qualified for their own job, do not have the tools necessary to make sure the nurses' duties are done 100 percent correctly.

This conundrum leads to an increase in risk for the district. The reason for this increase in risk is due to an untrained person doing a highly skilled person's duties. This increase in risk is straightforward; so what does tracking expenditures on nurses have to do with student achievement?

Simply put, a key to raising student achievement is noticeable learning or where a teacher can see the children's viewpoint about how learning should take place. The teacher then takes that information by using the methods the student used to teach themselves initially.

Nurses help with visible learning through having the child ready to learn by having any appropriate medication taken properly. Nurses also help by recommending a child to go home when he is sick, thereby preventing the spread of illness. If a child is under the weather then she is in no shape or form to learn. In other words the nurse makes sure the child is healthy enough to engage in learning necessary to be successful.

Social Workers

To round out the four positions the social workers track the external environment and helps if the child needs placement elsewhere or a way out of their current living situation. The most indirect position mentioned here is however they still play a vital role and are worth every penny.

In reference to student achievement, social workers have the least relative position, but they are necessary for the entire student body to be successful and the administrator can turn over cases to the social workers to investigate so that he or she can focus his or her attention on being the instructional leader.

Most importantly, the social worker is the voice of the students who are vulnerable and need extra specialized attention. Remember it is the districts' responsibility to educate these children also. There is an inherent, role for the social worker as they have a direct correlation to a specific population, those students who need a voice the most.

If the expenditure data changes in a negative way, the district leaders need to worry about what external environments are affecting their children because there is less help available. Furthermore, training is needed for social workers because the external environment for a child is very fluid.

CONCLUSION

For lasting district success, the EC students' needs should be met. However, their needs can be very expensive and constant planning and monitoring needs to go into the EC budget to prevent a balloon effect. That ballooning of expenditures could leave the district in a non-favorable position where the district would need to divert funds from another area to cover the unexpected expenditures.

Testing is the main communicator for the successes and opportunities of the district. The testing department can be monitored through expenditures to make sure the department is still running as a well-oiled machine.

The saying is always thrown around, from a book written by a former first lady, that it takes a village. That is a true statement but to look at the saying more in depth, the mental health workers make sure the children can deal with any adversity they may be going through to learn and exceed.

Guidance counselors work with the children as they transition through grades and character development. Nurses focus on the actual health of the children. Finally the social worker is there in case there needs to be any intervention between the environment at home and the well-being of the child.

Mental health workers, guidance counselors, nurses, and social workers are four very different positions that are critical to student achievement. There are pros to increasing funding and major pitfalls for decreasing funding. All of these increases or decreases in expenditures can predict the future if they are examined on a year-by-year basis or benchmarking a district with similar demographics. In this case it not only takes a village but it takes a fully funded staff.

Chapter 10

What Expenditures Directly Correlate with Student Achievement

Operating a school district is big business. Each district has almost the exact same departments as a major corporation (human resources and finance, to name a few). These departments have a correlation with student achievement.

In this chapter, seven areas are examined and how the expenditure data can be interpreted to predict student achievement. It is important to realize how every dollar spent needs to be broken down and analyzed on a per-pupil basis.

TUTORS

Tutors can be a missing link to help students excel academically. An important piece is the relationship that is built with the students due to a one-on-one interaction. Quite frankly tutoring is a necessity because it is the only way (one-to-one instruction) some students can learn.

Tutoring expenditures tend to be the first on the chopping block when budget cuts come down the pipe. Measuring the per-pupil expenditures is the simplest way to see if tutoring is happening in the district and consequently in the schools.

Tutoring can be seasonal; therefore, it is important to benchmark the schools against themselves year after year and to pull the specific date range that is being compared. Once the per-school amount is determined, create a per-pupil average for the entire district (dividing the expenditures by the total students in the district); this exercise could also be performed at each academic level (elementary and secondary).

Once the average is completed, a decision can be made at a glance whether there needs to be a higher investment in tutoring to maintain current academic performance.

If academic performance is satisfactory in school year 2014–2015 and the total tutoring expenditures were 100K or $20 per child for that: a district which that has 5,000 children, with 35K or $7 spent by December of 2014. However, in 2015–2016, 10K or $2 per child is spent in December of 2015 for the entire district. The district would need to ask, why the decrease? Because if tutoring is down, then academic performance could also be down and before the final grades are recorded, a renewed effort can be made toward offering tutoring and the benefits it gives the district can be realized.

HUMAN RESOURCES

The pure function of the human resources department is to help facilitate the supervising (evaluation), hiring, firing, and pay scale creation and implementation for all employees. HR effects students directly through its relationship with the staff and the staff's evaluation.

A robust teacher evaluation system is critical to district success. Evaluations take a critical look at how the teacher is performing. A necessary step is an initial self-assessment because the way the teacher sees himself or herself may need to be calibrated.

Then that view can be built upon by the supervisor through the supervisor's evaluation. Empathy is a key component to educating children and self-awareness is a key to empathy.

Relationships are critical here because the teacher receiving the feedback must trust the supervisor giving it. Therefore, it is important for the supervisor that conducts the evaluation to have integrity in the eyes of the teacher or person being evaluated. The integrity creates trust and can move the teacher forward if there is a need for improvement.

The reason the evaluation is so important is because it is the main way that teachers can get better. It also helps to measure the strength of the district as a whole. Furthermore, if academic performance is dropping and the evaluations are coming back with flying remarks, then there may be a disconnect between the evaluation process and the actual results of student achievement.

Professional development to calibrate the evaluation process can be measured through professional development expenditures and supplies and materials relative to the department responsible to giving said staff development program.

Recruitment is another key function of human resources. In rural areas teacher turnover can be higher; therefore, recruitment is critical to keep the teaching force whole. To track this look at the travel expenditure data within the specific HR department budgets. The travel costs are incurred from traveling to different job fairs and recruitment events.

As mentioned earlier one of the keys to student achievement is consistency and to achieve consistency is to have a whole teacher force. Of course, there is going to be maternity leaves and sickness. However, if the majority of the teacher force is whole, then the routine absences can be managed, but if there are more number of vacancies and routine absences on top of that, then there is a significant problem.

Admittedly there is little financial correlation between the HR department and student achievement, but the teacher evaluation process is so critical that correlating the evaluation results to student achievement is the same principle as monitoring per-pupil expenditures to predict student achievement.

FINANCE

This entire book revolves around the relationship between finance and student achievement. However, there is another aspect of the finance department that contributes to student achievement. Those aspects can be broken down into two pieces: payroll (how the employees are paid) and accounts payable (where the vendors get paid).

Looking at the payroll piece first, customer service is critical, because if a person has a question about his or her pay and it is not solved immediately, then those thoughts will linger with that person. It is only human nature that this worry occurs if an instant answer isn't obtained about a pay check discrepancy. It is human nature because it could affect the person's perception of survival.

Therefore, if a teacher calls in with a problem or concern with his or her take-home pay and it is not resolved in a timely manner then the teacher, by human nature, will continue to worry about his or her take-home pay and not the students he or she is responsible for. Since this is human nature the burden of this responsibility lands on the finance department.

The department should have things in place to offer exceptional customer service. Furthermore, the mission of the finance department should center around serving its stakeholders.

Even though customer service sometimes cannot happen immediately, it is important to remember that there is a reputation or a confidence that the finance department will deliver results within a certain amount of time.

Paying vendors is another point where the finance department can succeed and contribute to student achievement. Furthermore, the department is responsible for the timely delivery of products for the day-to-day operations of the district and things needed in a pinch. The business side of the school district lies here.

One thing that is relatively new is the use of purchasing cards or p-cards; many times they offer a high degree of fraud protection and a cashback feature. The cashback benefits the district, whereas the ease of use helps the vendors get paid faster as opposed to having the vendor wait for a paper check.

The way to maximize the performance of p-cards and keep their use satisfactory for an audit is to tie open purchase orders to the limit associated with each individual p-card. A purchase order is a universal form of pre-approval given from supervisors and/or budget managers to the person performing the actual process of purchasing the materials.

For example, if a department needs to purchase supplies in the amount of $500 in November, and they are going to use the p-card to purchase the supplies. Then the department would open a purchase order for $500 and the limit of the p-card would be set for $500 in November. This purchase order and p-card limit reconciliation is a monthly process.

There can be additional purchase orders added to the same card, and the sum of those purchase orders would be the total of the limit on the p-card. The reason for this reconciliation and alignment of purchase orders and credit limits is to lower the amount of risk for the school district.

If the open limits of the p-cards match the combined credit limits of the p-cards, then the district has prior approval for all of their open credit.

Finally to measure the performance and track use the district leaders could look not at expenditures but revenue per pupil for the rebate amount from the p-card. They could also look at the expenditures on a monthly basis to monitor the use.

The use is important because it shows that vendors are getting paid quickly which leads to a steady flow of supplies and materials for the students to use, which should be facilitating learning.

There may be a district lead staff development program where the materials may be delivered late or may have been forgotten to be ordered. A good relationship with timely payments with a vendor can help correct that oversight by providing the materials needed at the last minute.

Switching to the actual business side of it, the finance department is the point of contact to conduct the audit, which leads to other opportunities or missed opportunities if the audit comes back less than positive.

The audit is the report card for how the school district spends its funds relative to the local, state, and federal guidelines. Audits are looked at to gauge the financial health of the district along with the ability of the district to spend their funds properly. The audit also tells the story to grantors if the district can spend their grant awards properly.

CLERICAL

Please remember that parent involvement is a key to moving a school forward and hence a district forward! One of the key ways to have parents participate is to provide excellent customer service. Customer service starts with the leaders, a tone at the top, but it is executed by the clerical staff.

It is important to monitor the cost of clerical expense because the general public has a difficult time conceptualizing the link between the need for clerical staff and student achievement. A lot of decisions are made in the general public by perception. However, the link between student achievement and the amount spent on clerical staff is real. A key component to calming an irate parent down is listening and showing empathy.

The critical piece is calming the parent down initially and nothing infuriates a parent more than getting an automated message. Therefore, it is important to make the investment in clerical staff, to make sure the school or department has enough coverage to help smooth out the parent complaints by, simply, having a person to answer the phone.

If there are drastic cuts needed and it is deemed that clerical staff is indeed cut, then focus on parent volunteers to help answer the phones so that, even though the funds are cut, there can still be excellent customer service.

Consequently it is critical to hold clerical expense relatively flat on a per-pupil basis as long as the customer service is viewed as high quality. How can a school measure customer service? The most direct way would be to send a survey. Most schools have a sign-in system and with that the school could request the email address of the person/guest entering the school.

Once the school has the email address, it can send a survey that questions if the participant received great customer service. The survey can include a variety of other questions but the main theme could be related to customer service.

If the process could be automated where the parent signs in electronically and then a survey is automatically sent to their inbox, it would require no work on the part of the school, and they could record and disseminate the data.

TEACHER ASSISTANTS

A highly debated topic is the need for teacher assistants (TAs) in a classroom or too just a lower class size. Either way the district needs one or the other. Therefore, if spending per pupil on TAs is decreasing, then the expenditure amount on classroom teachers should be rising to compensate if the staffing level was appropriate to begin with.

TAs can be used in variety of different ways. They can be assigned to individual classrooms or they could float along grade levels. However, it is important that they are utilized in an instructionally sound manner and viewed as instructional assistants. It is easy to fall into the trap of using TAs as office help for filing or as other noninstructional help.

In a high-poverty district the instructional staff ratio to students needs to remain relatively low for several reasons. The first reason is relationships; the students need to build a caring relationship with an adult who cares about them.

Second with the word count gap being so high with students when they arrive in kindergarten, it is critical that they get one-on-one instruction to help close that gap. If that gap is not closed in a timely manner, absenteeism and discipline issues are not far behind.

Third, with high poverty, there tends to be a disproportionality problem between certain demographics in poverty and suspension and discipline issues. Having a low staff to child ratio, especially in the early years can help even out those suspensions around demographics, because the staff can create a relationship with their students.

It goes without saying that the more students a teacher has without an assistant, the lower the probability that the teacher will be able to build relationships with the students. Think of the relationships as lighter fluid. When lighting charcoal on a grill, the flame will die out before the charcoal gets hot enough to cook the food. However, by adding lighter fluid, the flame will act as a catalyst to make the charcoals hot enough to cook.

If a teacher tries to teach, it will catch with some students some of the time, but if the teacher develops relationships, then the teaching and learning will take hold and work through boredom, which will translate into less negative behaviors. Therefore, less funding for TAs and less relationships, built between a teacher and a student, will lead to a downward trend in student achievement.

SOFTWARE

The first step in deciding to invest in software is to line up the software to the strategic plan. Does the software accomplish a plan, goal, or objective? The second step to is determine a return on investment (ROI). Traditionally ROI is measured in pure dollars; however, in this case it could be measured in results.

It takes time to gather district data because there needs to be at least two years data to compare. Therefore, it could be a possibility that the district pays for two years of software—which may be useless—unless the data that is being measured is independent of the software.

For example, if math scores are low in an end-of-grade test and the standards stay the same, then the software could be measured with one year of use. The deciding factor would be: Did math scores go up? If not, then a justification could be made to terminate the math software program.

Using software expenditures to predict student achievement is a multistep process. If there is a drop in per-pupil spending (the total spending on software divided by the number of children in the district) and there has been an increase in student performance, this downturn in expenditures could lead to detrimental effects on student achievement.

The following are some of the possible scenarios:

- If the previous two years' test scores are flat or down, then there should be a downtrend in the per-pupil expenditure and then an uptrend in per-pupil software expenditures. This scenario shows that software has been discontinued because it was ineffective and new software was purchased to help with the declining scores.
- If test scores are up, then the per-pupil software expenditures should follow; this shows that the investment is paying off and is continuing to be made.
- If spending is up, down, then up again, there probably was an inventory or reconciliation done of the software programs and the ones that are not aligned with the districts needs were discontinued and new ones were implemented.

Finally, software can be expensive and ineffective. Therefore, all software programs need to be reconciled year after year to check for relevancy and effectiveness. Costs will go down if the software is discontinued, but achievement should stay flat because of the ineffectiveness of the software.

It is similar to paying for a landline at a personal residence when the people that live there all have cell phones. The landline was there, but really not that effective because everyone has cell phones. Therefore, discontinuing the landline isn't going to affect anything, except to save money.

PRE-K

Pre-K is one of the cornerstones to high student achievement. Cost associated with Pre-K would be the teacher and TA salaries, supplies, materials, contracted services, and clerical.

It is imperative that the cost per pupil remains flat or increases because that means there are more resources being devoted to an important program. Pre-K is important because it can help children who are starting late catch up and lay the groundwork for a successful academic career.

Investments in Pre-K have been shown to reduce the number of dropouts and discipline issues. Therefore, it seems like an investment in Pre-K would be a no brainer. A lot of times the data, test scores, from Pre-K are tracked where the expenditures are not.

It is such an important part of the district that it should be examined routinely to make sure the investment is being made. A conversation about district initiatives should be about Pre-K–12 as opposed to K–12.

The district should have a passion for their Pre-K department because outside the funds that are invested, the Pre-K program has the most upside or potential to show positive gains for the district as a whole. There is, however, no instant reward and that could be a hurdle to jump over when comparing investments to Pre-K over another option that may show results faster.

CONCLUSION

Monitoring other expenditures deepens the understanding of what kind of performance the district will have. Furthermore, all programs lead to the overall success of the district, which is a school system and not a system of schools. This approach keeps every student in mind.

Each department contributes in its own way to the performance of the district. It is important for the leadership of the district to understand which way the contribution is going. If the per-pupil expenditures are going south at a particular time, then the leaders can see where they need to compensate other services because they will know how that respective department contributes to the overall education of the student.

Chapter 11

Linking the Strategic Plan to Budget

INTRODUCTION

It is important to have a plan to move a school district forward. This plan should have a five-year or long focus range and short-term measurable goals to track the progress. Finally everything the district does should reflect the plan.

There should be a link between this plan and everything the district does (budgets, meeting agendas, and other district plans), for both long and short terms. Luckily most districts have a plan like this; it is their strategic plan (SP). Every agenda and every budget should mirror the SP.

WHY IS THE SP SO IMPORTANT?

The SP is the road map for the district. The SP is prepared by involving community stakeholders, employees, and elected officials. Therefore, the SP should have the engagement from all of those groups.

The engagement is the critical piece to the puzzle of the political side of the business of the school district. If the district has the engagement from the stakeholders, employees, and elected officials and the budget matches the SP, then the stakeholders, employees, and elected officials have already approved the budget.

Imagine the power of the budget being pre-approved before it is even presented to the stakeholders, employees, and elected officials. Take a one-to-one initiative if it is detailed in the SP by having specific language about using a digital delivery method for classroom instruction. Then the expenditure for this specific project should be approved without any problem.

The necessity to have a plan when managing a major project is well documented. When working in a large organization, such as a school district, a formal plan or outline for the direction of the organization is a must.

Additionally having a SP helps every department stay on track or within the mission of the school district. Very easily a department or school could view themselves as operating in a silo or independent of the district.

Every department should be asked to hold themselves accountable for every action by literally linking the actions of the department to the SP. By doing so, it should become routine to have a presentation or an update of a certain department and how the actions and directions taken by that department are linked to the SP.

Simplified SP (example)—
Goal 4—Efficient Functioning Learning Environments
Objective 1—Maintain safe and clean schools
Objective 2—Schools have supplies and materials to facilitate an orderly and clean school building
Objective 3—Staff will receive training to maximize tasks and to understand and utilize new technology

Sample Budget

Table 11.1 details an example of a simplified goal from a SP and the budget that corresponds with it. Notice the main premise of the goal is clean and safe schools and the staff and training is also listed.

The key part to notice is how the SP and the budget are linked together. Another example of the same goal in the SP is focusing on the district—creating a safe place for all of its students. It could be a best practice for the maintenance department to make a mid-year presentation on how the installation of security cameras is going throughout the district and how the installations of the cameras relates to the goal of the SP that talks about creating a safe environment. Preparing the narrative to the budget for the security cameras to look similar to the above objectives which link this particular SP goal and the budget together.

If there is a new technology or activity that comes up but was not covered in the plan, it would be advisable to edit the plan to fit the new activity.

Table 11.1 Sample Budget

Budget Code	Description	Budget Amount	SP Goal and Objective
1.5110.007.181	Custodial pay	25,450.00	Goal 4 Objective 3
1.5110.007.411	Supplies and materials	12,330.00	Goal 4 Objective 2
1.5110.007.312	Workshop expense	1,650.00	Goal 4 Objective 2

For example, if a district was looking to go one-to-one and realizes that there are no sufficient internet locations for children to do their homework, then it provides free internet access and there is nothing in the SP about making sure there is internet access available to all students outside of the school building.

It would be advisable to change the plan to match this new project that needs to be facilitated. An additional benefit of adding the new activity to the SP is that it creates a vetting process for the new activity.

Also if there are exceptions made to the SP, then that sends a message of inconsistency to the district and the employees will pick up on the inconsistency. Since the SP starts at the top, it would be necessary to implement a proper protocol so that the message of compliance is nonverbally communicated throughout the district, a classic tone at the top.

Back to the lack of internet locations, the goal or part of a goal needs to state that external factors affecting outside school expectations should be looked at and a solution created or making sure that all students have equitable opportunities to compete on the same academic playing field.

Now not only is that goal going to be vetted properly, but adding the goal creates an transparent sense of operations. A group can be assigned from the initial group of the stakeholders, employees, and elected officials to meet about adding new goals to plan.

OVERVIEW OF LINKING THE SP TO THE DAY-TO-DAY OPERATIONS

Agendas are an important function of every meeting, especially if the meeting is to be successful and meaningful. Every topic on every agenda should link back to the SP. It should physically say on the agenda how each topic links back to the SP.

For example, if there is a goal in the SP that focuses on reducing teacher turnover, then the staff development program for the principals could focus on reducing teacher turnover by training the principals to mentor or provide more support for beginning teachers (a group where teacher turnover tends to be higher), then the agenda next to the item being presented would state the goal and number so that everyone is clear on what the expectation is.

Every plan that is created should link back to the SP. For clarification every department should at the minimum have a vision and mission statement. Some departments will have specific plans. For example, career and technical education will have a separate plan. Most programs which receive federal funding will have their own plans.

Grant applications fall under this umbrella as well. There can be very specific data required to stay in compliance with certain grants and that language should match the SP.

Every budget should link back to a program plan that would have a direct link back to the SP. For example, a title I plan may talk about lowering class because it provides optimal learning environments for a-trisk children. There should be a goal in the SP that references creating optimal learning environments.

Finally the expenditures in the title I budget for classroom teachers and the resulting data (class size numbers) will be the final piece to bring that information full circle for the plan itself.

There also needs to be a follow-up piece that relates the data back to the expenditure and ultimately back to the SP. For the example of lowering class size with title I dollars, did student achievement increase, remain flat, or decrease? That answer will help the district know if they should continue to make that investment.

When the budget is prepared, the SP should be referenced heavily and there should be a presentation of both documents. One document is the SP that shows how much money is actually spent on each goal, for example, creation and fostering of a safe environment—$250,000. This reflects a $250,000 investment in security cameras for safety at the schools.

This is accurate if in the budget there is $250,000 set aside for a safe environment. The budget may have a different title for the area that the actual expenditure may come out of. For example, it may be called cameras.

Next the budget should show which goal is associated with the expenditure by line item. Letters and number can be used to simplify the process. Simplicity is the key so that nonfinancial types are not overwhelmed.

For example, looking again at the goal of creating a safe environment, let's say the goal is number 3 safe and nurturing schools and the objective number is 5 for the actual safety piece. The budget would read: 2.6550.069.411 Security Cameras $250,000.00 (budgeted amount) SP goal 3 obj. 1.

It needs to be ingrained into the culture of the school district that this type of data arrangement is done with every presentation. Even to the level when a department is asking for additional resources, they should have the goal number.

That way it can make a difficult process of making sure the funding matches the plan simplified by having the person requesting or in charge of the funding doing the heavy lifting of matching the expenditures before approval is given for new or current activities.

HOW TO MAKE THE BUDGET MATCH THE SP

The first step in having the SP match the budget is to make the goal in for the SP. Once the goal is made, it important to dissect it to see where the budget can be used to help contribute to make the goal possible. In other words strip the goal down to manageable pieces and see if those pieces need money to be executed.

For example, take a goal like decreasing the dropout rate by 5 percent by 2021 and it is currently 2016. The first thing to decide is if the goal is going to be to decrease the drop rate by 1 percent every year over the next five years to get to the total goal of 5 percent or if there is just a notion that somewhere over the five years the district will reduce the dropout rate.

Next, look at what things go into decreasing the dropout rate, or what contributes to the dropout rate. For example, absenteeism is a leading indicator for a potential dropout. How can a district use money to lower absenteeism?

Finally, determine what can be purchased to lower absenteeism, it could range from adding staff to professional development to facilitate building relationships with students. Either way that expenditure can be directly linked to the SP.

To take this a step further, if there were funds available, it could be taken to the board that governs the district and presented that there needs to be an addition of staff to lower absenteeism and once the connection is made between lower absenteeism and how that lowers the dropout rate then the board should have no problem approving the additional staff.

To finish out this example, the 2016 five-year SP would look like this:

Goal 1—Reduce Dropout Rate

Objective 1—By 2021 Anywhere the school district will lower the dropout rate by 5 percent—the target goal will be to reduce the dropout rate by 1 percent every year. Cost—1 attendance counselor $50,000 per year.

The budget would look like this:
2.5110.002.131—Other Counselor SP 1-1

Notice that even though the example is not specifically detailed (it takes way more than an attendance counselor to lower the dropout rate), the SP and budget show the appropriate data as to how much it takes to accomplish the goal and how the line item in the budget contributes to the SP.

The SP is the district's road map to accomplish its respective goals and the budget should be correlated with this road map. If there are any expenditures that do not relate to the road map, they should not be executed. There may be extreme circumstances but, as mentioned earlier, the SP should be amended to match the new expenditure.

CONCLUSION

The key to unlocking the power of the SP is to have a lot of people on the committee to create the SP. They need to be stakeholders, employees, and elected officials. Having their buy-in from the beginning can help pave the way for the district success.

Linking the SP to the budget is a critical process because it puts the district's money where its mouth is. All agendas should link back to the SP, and the two should mirror each other. The agendas and budgets should actually list the SP goals and objectives in a simple way that is crystal clear for everyone involved, indicating which part of the SP that the respective document is reflecting.

If there is an addition or request and it is not on the strategic or part of an amendment, then it should be turned down. The SP is the list of goals that the district wants to accomplish; therefore, having the budget match the SP helps ensure the district is using its resources to accomplish its goals.

Chapter 12

How It All Fits Together

Bringing this book to an end signals the beginning of a new journey. Here, it is important to summarize all the tools presented in this book. It is significant to understand the underlying theme. The finance department has audited financial data that can be used to predict student achievement. The idea of having more data available to help predict student achievement will be very helpful in making a school district more successful.

Finance can no longer go without a seat at the table. Even though there are some downsides to running a government organization like a business, it is completely rational to look at the financial outcomes of a school district, from a business perspective, and take those recommended actions and reconcile them for what is best for the student.

WHAT IS THE BIG IDEA?

Three things need to be considered when trying to improve a school district or initiate a major change:

- What specifically is trying to be changed?
- What change might be introduced?
- How will the change be measured?

Financial data is perfect in relation to trying to view the actual change. This is true because it is simple to measure dollars and cents and compare them to previous years. Therefore, financial data is critical when making or initiating major change.

When taking a deeper look at what needs to be changed, the indicator or expenditure can be looked at. For example, if a district is looking to lower discipline referrals on the bus, there are several ways that this can be accomplished: adding more adults to the bus, staff development program for the bus drivers on how to build relationships with children, and adding Wi-Fi to the bus (Wi-Fi is just an illustration of giving the children something to do while on the bus).

All three can be measured with expenditure/financial data. More adults would be measured by comparing payroll data year after year. Staff development program and Wi-Fi would follow the same path, measuring the data year after year. For example, how much money was spent last year compared to how much money was spent this year.

It is critical that the idea of predicting student achievement is fully understood. Put simply, a district can sense what direction it is going by its expenditures. For example, how change can be done specifically, how it can be introduced, and how will it be measured; all these can be tracked through financial expenditures.

It is prudent that the finance department takes part in the conversation about educating a child. The finance department has a unique perspective and can offer insight. The insight usually relates to repetition because the finance department can see multiple services covering the same area.

They also can track the employee side by seeing if there has been a spike in hiring for a certain area. Furthermore, the finance department has a unique perspective on the leadership capabilities of senior staff members.

The finance department is driven by due dates and accuracy. If a principal or director is inept at handling these deadlines, then the finance department can see that. If the principal or director cannot handle the due dates, what else can they not handle?

Let's build on the point of the principal or director not meeting finance's deadlines or cooperating by taking the following into consideration: money is one of the most common things that can get an administrator fired.

This is no secret that money has the special power to have someone lose their career in education. Therefore, if an administrator cannot handle those duties, it truly says a lot about his or her prioritization skill set.

In the words of Albert Einstein, "Anyone who doesn't take truth seriously in small matters cannot be trusted in large ones either." If an administrator cannot handle deadlines or tasks that could very easily get him or her fired, then what else is he or she not handling properly?

LIVING IN THE PAST

"Those who do not remember the past are condemned to repeat it."

—George Santayana

Looking at past expenditures is the key to the whole notion of using the past to predict the future. However, the budget is also a useful tool. The sweet spot is when the budget and past expenditures are reconciled to see if any change has been made to past patterns.

This means that if a district has a new initiative, did the district change its budget to reflect the new initiative? If it did not, then the initiative must not have a great deal of importance. Almost every change requires money to do it, even if it is just training. Remember, sending someone to training has several components: travel, hotel stay, per-diem, possible air fare, and substitute teacher costs. Therefore, even if it is just training, there would be budget changes associated with it.

The idea of changing the budget to facilitate change can be viewed at 50,000 feet by various stakeholders. When a new budget is created, it usually has the previous year's numbers listed next to the new year's number. Therefore, it is simple to see if there is a change in the budget.

Also, a tool would be useful to explain changes that happen year after year in the budget. For example, if computer purchases rise 10 percent, it could be listed that it is the first refresh year for a one-to-one initiative.

For most states, school district budgets are public knowledge; therefore, anyone could request the budget and review it for themselves. Transparency is key when dealing with tax payers' dollars.

SIMPLICITY IN REPORTING

"Simplicity is the ultimate sophistication."

—Leonardo da Vinci

To have an at-a-glance view of the district's efficiency indicators becomes the lynchpin to spending funds in the best way possible. Some financial data cannot be translated into indicators for student achievement. For the data that can be translated, simplicity in presentation is critical. Therefore, if the data being communicated from the finance department is not being communicated in simple ways, there is issue with that.

Almost all financial data can be used to make sure spending is maximized. There are a couple of ways that this can be achieved and that is by benchmarking another school district that has the same demographics and is successful or by comparing the district against itself for the same relative time period.

These numbers can be presented with a line graph to see which way the trend is heading. Remember, the per-pupil amount is critical because a lot of a school district's funds are allocated based on how many pupils they have and the numbers of pupils fluctuates year after year.

The per-pupil amount is a relative figure that can be used to look at the expenditure data to see if there has been any increase, and in case of any increase, what has contributed to it. Reconciling the increases can help bring down expense, leaving more funds for the core mission of the district.

WHAT TO COUNT

> "Not everything that counts can be counted and not everything that can be counted counts."
>
> —Albert Einstein

When looking at millions of dollars of expenditures, it is important to realize what the actual target of the investigation is. It is critical to break down the problem to see its contributed factors.

For example, if a district is trying to figure out why science scores have dropped, then the first step would be to ferret out the potential reasons.

- Lack of certified classroom teacher—Substitute teacher costs
- Lack of an experienced teacher—Decrease in salary expense but the position count remains the same
- Lack of deliverables for the students—Decrease in instructional supply expense as it is related to the science department
- Lack of engagement on the part of the student—Decrease in technology purchases for the science department

The critical factor and example is that the cost of electricity for the science building was not mentioned. Monitoring utility expenditures is critical to maximizing district funds, but it is not as helpful as looking at academic growth.

Therefore, dig deep into the problem, find the contributing factors, see which of those factors have a cost associated with the contributing factor, and then benchmark or compare the cost to other sources.

AUXILIARY SERVICES

> "It's the little details that are vital. Little things make the big things happen."
>
> —John Wooden

Observing auxiliary services (technology, maintenance, transportation, and child nutrition) for spending efficiency is a little process that can pay big dividends. These departments take a lot of funding, and they need to be monitored for efficiency and potential savings opportunities.

Many examples have been given in this book, but it is important to remember that a lot of times a district needs money to start or improve an initiative. A lot of times new money is not available; therefore, looking at the funding the district has is the only option.

Finally, there is a lot of opportunity in auxiliary services through process improvements and for more efficient pieces of equipment. It is important to keep up to date on current trends. A small investment could save millions, freeing up those millions for curriculum and instruction.

TOOLS OF THE TRADE

> "One of my primary objects is to form the tools so the tools themselves shall fashion the work and give to every part it's just portion."
>
> —Eli Whitney

District leaders can control the outcomes of the district by manipulating certain aspects of the budget. Think of it as controlling the amount of salt or pepper used in a recipe. Most school districts have the same plan or recipe.

However, some people like their meals just a bit different, so they may add more salt or pepper and vice versa. A school district may have more ESL students or higher poverty students.

These districts require more investment in certain aspects and the districts with the opposite needs have a little different tuning to do, or they need a little more or a little less salt and pepper.

An example for this is the beginning teacher department. If a district historically has more beginning teachers than the state average, it would be fair to assess that their expenditures in the beginning teacher department would be higher than a district that has a more experienced staff.

Therefore, it is perfectly rational that the district has this higher expenditure than average. What if the district had higher than average expenditures in their beginning teacher department but not a higher than average beginning teacher population? Then there is a mismatch, and that needs to be investigated.

Taking this example to the next level, look at the past to see if the district used to have a history of high beginning teacher turnover or population and now it does not. That could be a function of a highly effective beginning teacher department. Now comes the clincher; since the turnover has gone down, ratchet down the expenditures and divert that money somewhere else that needs it within the strategic plan.

It is counterintuitive to cut the budget of a department that is successful, but the department has done its job and should be recognized for that. It is time to move the money to another source to maximize student achievement. Money can be a zero-sum game, where the only place to get it is to take it from somewhere else.

Constant monitoring and changing is critical to keep up to date and continue to not only be good stewards of tax payers' money but also give the children what they need.

PUTTING THE DISTRICTS MONEY WHERE ITS MOUTH IS

> "A good plan violently executed now is better than a perfect plan executed next week."
>
> —George S. Patton

Every budget and agenda in a school district should mirror the strategic plan. The strategic plan is the road map for the district to accomplish its goals. The agendas of the meetings the district has are the vehicle, and the budget is the gas to drive the vehicle.

If for some reason the path to student success takes another turn than was initially planned, it is fine because the agendas and budget can be amended. Another key factor is the amount of stakeholders involved in the creation of the strategic plan.

If those stakeholders approve the strategic plan and the budget matches it, then in theory the budget has already been approved because the plan associated with the budget has stakeholder buy-in already. This is a powerful tool, especially when additional or new money is needed. The trick is to make sure the people who have a say in granting new money for the district are part of the group to build and approve the strategic plan.

CONCLUSION

The goal of this book is to give the reader a practical and understandable guide on how to use readily available financial information and use that data to predict student achievement.

Everyone who works in education has one goal, and that it to help our children succeed. Not all will go on to college—and that is acceptable. But it is necessary that we use the available data to help make their lives better.

Educators and administrators cannot be complacent because the final outcome is the future. With school districts being among the largest expenditures state and local governments have, it is imperative that all the plans, budgets, and expenditures match, and that there has been a significant amount of planning given to figuring out how to best prepare the road map for the future. Because state and local governments are counting on the school districts to deliver a significant return on investment.

Finally with the rise of charter schools, home schooling, the privatization of schools, and private schools (and the vouchers associated with using state dollars to pay for private schools), the competition is rising greatly. Therefore, public schools need to use their tools to gain a competitive advantage and that advantage is the finance department.

About the Author

Jay C. Toland has been in public school finance for seven years. He is currently the chief financial officer for Scotland County Schools in Laurinburg, North Carolina. He has been with Scotland County Schools since 2012. Since 2012 Scotland County Schools have been awarded the Certificate of Achievement for Excellence in Financial Reporting (2012–2013, 2013–2014, and 2014–2015) from the Government Finance Officers Association, the Certificate of Excellence in Financial Reporting (2012–2013, 2013–2014, and 2014–2015) from the Association of Schools Business Officials, the Meritorious Budget Award (2015–2016) also from the Association of School Business Officials, and the Award of Excellence of Financial Reporting from the State Board of Education of North Carolina (2012–2013, 2013–2014, and 2014–2015).

Jay graduated from Louisburg College with an associate degree in arts, the University of North Carolina at Wilmington with a bachelor of science in management, the University of North Carolina at Pembroke with a masters degree in business administration, and East Carolina University with a graduate certificate in hospitality management and another graduate certificate in finance.

Jay is a certified management accountant from the International Association of Management Accountants, a certified administrator of school finance and operations from the Association of School Business Officials, and a certified schools business director from the North Carolina Association of School Business Officials.

He currently resides in Raeford, North Carolina, with his wife Mackenzie and daughter Adaline.

www.ingramcontent.com/pod-product-compliance
Lightning Source LLC
Chambersburg PA
CBHW030146240426
43672CB00005B/293